Contemporary
One-Act Plays

Selected and Introduced

by

JAMES REDMOND
Lecturer in English, Westfield College, London University

and

HALLAM TENNYSON
Assistant Head of Radio Drama, BBC

Published for the
English Association by
HEINEMANN EDUCATIONAL BOOKS

Heinemann Educational Books Ltd
Halley Court, Jordan Hill, Oxford OX2 8EJ
OXFORD LONDON EDINBURGH
MADRID ATHENS BOLOGNA
MELBOURNE SYDNEY AUCKLAND
IBADAN NAIROBI GABORONE HARARE
KINGSTON PORTSMOUTH (NH) SINGAPORE

ISBN 0 435 23723 3

Introduction and Selection
Heinemann Educational Books 1976
First published 1976
Reprinted 1980, 1983, 1986, 1988

Filmset in 10/11 Garamond by
Spectrum Typesetting Ltd, London
Printed in Great Britain by
Richard Clay Ltd, Bungay, Suffolk

Contents

Acknowledgements

The English Association and the publishers are indebted to the following for permission to reprint the undermentioned plays:

Faber & Faber Ltd for *Play* by Samuel Beckett.

Jonathan Cape Ltd for *The Zoo Story* by Edward Albee from *The Zoo Story and Other Plays*.

Eyre Methuen Ltd for *Revue Sketches* by Harold Pinter from *A Slight Ache and Other Plays*, © Harold Pinter 1961.

Faber & Faber Ltd for *If You're Glad, I'll be Frank* by Tom Stoppard.

The BBC for *On a Day in Summer in a Garden* by Don Haworth.

A. D. Peters & Company for *Marble Arch* by John Mortimer.

Introduction

What these plays have in common is that they are short. There are no rules in this business, and a play may be exactly as long as a piece of string. A play, in my view, is as apt a description of Harold Pinter's five-minute contribution to the revue, *One to Another,* as it is for *Man and Superman* or the entire *Dance of Death*. No one complains about a Rembrandt etching because it is not the same size as Frith's 'Derby Day', nor do those who visit the National Gallery to revive their spirits with a look at Cézanne's 'Old Lady' grumble because that experience has occupied them for less than two solid hours.

This passage comes from John Mortimer's introduction to a collection of his own short plays, and it serves usefully as an epigraph for the present volume. Mr Mortimer turns naturally to painting for his analogy, because in common with painters the dramatist has the task of creating memorable images. The plays in this volume invite a wide range of emotional reactions; there are moments of frivolity, of *ennui*, of loathing nausea, of baffling ecstasy; but whether the mood is relaxed or taut the play will be successful for any reader or member of an audience to the extent that it offers him some picture which recurringly engages his imagination. Harold Pinter defines his own kind of theatre in terms that apply to all the plays in this volume when he speaks of the *compulsive* dramatic image, the concrete and particular picture of human life which commands 'active and willing participation', which demands of the reader or spectator that he should come to live with it. These plays do not take up many pages of print, but they are brought together as representative examples of how contemporary playwrights working in English have created images which compel attention.

John Mortimer, in continuing the analogy between the two art forms, might be speaking for each of the playwrights in this volume:

A play, even if it lasts not more than five minutes, should be able to contain at least one life, with a character that can be conceived as stretching backwards and forwards in time, with an existence longer than those moments which actually take place on the stage. A play is a demonstration, in which an audience can recognize something about themselves. As with a picture, this can be achieved by a few lines in the right position.

Samuel Beckett's *Play* was first performed in German in the Ulmer Theater, Ulm-Donau, West Germany, in June 1963. The English première was given by the National Theatre Company at The Old Vic in April 1964. Beckett's first intention was that the play should be acted twice in a meticulously identical form. That unprecedented stage direction 'Repeat play' (see p. 14) was to reset the cyclical action; and the closing of the repeat, with yet another return to the beginning (significantly, Beckett uses the musical term *da capo*), was to suggest an endless unchanging repetition. In the course of working on productions Beckett came to prefer a slightly changed repeat, one which would indicate not an immutable permanence, but an evolving context, an existence gradually crumbling towards darkness and silence. In a letter to George Devine, who directed the National Theatre production, Beckett explained his final thoughts on how the repeat might best be presented:

We now think it would be dramatically more effective to have it express a slight weakening, both of question and of response, by means of less and perhaps slower light and correspondingly less volume and speed of voice . . . The impression of falling off which this would give, with suggestion of conceivable dark and silence in the end, or of an indefinite approximating towards it, would be reinforced if we obtained also, in the repeat, a quality of hesitancy, of both question and answer, perhaps not so much in a slowing down of actual débit as in a less confident movement of spot from one face to another and less immediate reaction of the voices . . . The inquirer (light) begins to emerge as no less a victim of his inquiry than they and as needing to be free, within narrow limits, literally to act the part, ie to vary if only slightly his speeds and intensities.

The force of this short play depends upon the success with which it brings together extremely contrasting dramatic impulses. On one level the action incorporates the effects aimed at in traditional bedroom farce, and the audience will laugh at moments in the way it would if the play were by Georges Feydeau. On another level there are the sad domestic pain and the emotional blundering of the three personalities involved: this aspect of the play asks for responses similar to those invited by Terence Rattigan in *The Deep Blue Sea* or by John Osborne in *Look Back in Anger*. The third level on which the play operates is one of metaphysical speculation: always, accompanying the irony of the *farceur* and the empathy of the playwright portraying emotional pain, there is the deeply reflective anguish that invites comparison with Dante, or Kafka, or T.S. Eliot. In bringing this curiously rich mixture of responses together, Beckett introduced to the modern theatre the complexity which had characterized his own fiction and that of his friend James Joyce.

The Zoo Story, Edward Albee's first play, was premièred in German at the Schiller Theater in Berlin in September 1959. It was first performed in English in a double bill with Beckett's *Krapp's Last Tape* at the Provincetown Playhouse in Greenwich Village, New York. Albee has expressed his consciousness of the play's debt to some playwrights he admires—Eugene O'Neill and Tennessee Williams as well as Beckett—but the peculiar mixture of religious longings, surface wit, self-debasement and obscenity is characteristic of Albee's contribution to American drama. Like the playwrights who have influenced him, he offers his work as 'drama of emotion and atmosphere' rather than 'drama of ideas'. He has constantly rejected critical approaches which have looked in his plays for allegorical meanings which can be precisely explicated: 'A play that is meant to be taken into the unconscious almost directly without being filtered through the brain cells can't be approached that way because you get stuck in specifics, stuck in allegory, stuck in symbols, and then you don't get the intended emotional impact'. *The Zoo Story* has a significant place in American drama not because of any ideas or arguments that might be read into it, but because it stays in the imagination as a complex structure of stage images and sounds, a compelling pattern of emotional and spiritual experience.

Harold Pinter's *Revue Sketches*, written between 1958 and 1964 reveal his talent for creating atmosphere through dialogue. This is indeed the strongest single element in his writing and when allied to a realistic narrative and a universal theme, as it is in *The Caretaker*, it has resulted in one of the few undoubted masterpieces of the contemporary British theatre. The revue sketches are incidents superbly observed and carried out with an exquisitely fine ear for the nuances of everyday London speech. Pinter's dialogue is not as purely naturalistic as has sometimes been suggested; we do not pause, stumble, leave loose ends, repeat ourselves or follow our own inner thought patterns to quite the same degree as Pinter's characters. In heightening these elements in the way he does, Pinter creates a poetry of the commonplace. Chekhov was perhaps the first dramatist to understand that our speech often serves to hide our true thoughts and feelings, rather than to reveal them. To be able to write dialogue which illustrates this gulf and which allows the audience to be aware of it is one of Pinter's great gifts. The sketches chosen here all show this quintessential Pinter characteristic: the brilliantly comic use of technical language ('they have gone vicious about the high speed taper shank spiral flute reamers') in *Trouble at the Works*, the banal pathos of the dialogue between the two derelict women in *Black and White*, and the repetitive mania of the lady in *Request Stop* are all employed with wit, economy and a masterly sense of timing.

Tom Stoppard's *If You're Glad, I'll be Frank* was his third play and as with the first two it was written for radio. The bus conductor who imagines his missing wife to be the speaking clock on the telephone and who pursues the phantom voice into the deepest recesses of the Ministry of Posts and Telegraphs, interrupting an ultra respectable boardroom meeting, is a superbly comic creation. But for all its zany humour and brilliant command of radio techniques it is much more than superficially amusing. It allows Stoppard to juggle with philosophical ideas in the manner that he has made peculiarly his own, but with a deftness and lightness of touch not always noticeable in his longer plays. The illusory nature of time, our fantastic inner imaginative life so sadly at odds with the strait-jacket of our urbanized, industrial environment—these are among the themes that emerge. The farce can be enjoyed at its face value, but for those who have ears to hear there is an unexpected depth and poignancy. Comedy has often been one of the best means of revealing the tragic pathos of human destiny, as Mozart showed in *Cosi Fan Tutte* where the music makes a universal statement about human passion through a story that on the surface seems little more than banal. *If You're Glad, I'll be Frank* once again performs such an act of transformation.

On a Day in Summer in a Garden was Don Haworth's twelfth play (all of them written for radio). It represented a radically new departure since most of his previous plays had all been brilliant variations on the traditional northern comedy—with refined landladies, erratic husbands, wild con-men (deceiving no one but themselves) all mixed together into a sort of steaming potato pie of pathos and absurdity from which the anti-hero, usually a peculiarly gormless northern innocent, emerged with his dignity strangely enhanced.

On a Day in Summer in a Garden, however, is a poetic fantasy: a conversation piece between three dock plants— gaffer, a young sprig and a seedling—in which they speculate on the absurdities of the human beings who are just on the point of making one of their periodic, death-dealing attacks. The play is gloriously funny, and touching and at the same time a shrewd comment on ecology. The human beings are only heard muttering gibberish in the distance—a gibberish which in the radio production was deliciously and pointedly accompanied by scraps of Mozart. Meanwhile the dock plants, bravely facing extinction, develop their own irresistible theories of human behaviour. To give but one example—human beings, so gaffer in his wisdom tells the youngest seedling, have only learned to use legs in order to be able to keep out of the way of falling cowpats: to move from such comedy as this to the haunting pathos of the end is a feat of considerable brilliance. Finally, this play is almost inconceivable outside the radio medium: if the dock plants were made visible the imagination would become clogged.

In *Marble Arch* John Mortimer offers a very skilful example of the *farceur*'s craft. In performance, the trick is for the director and actors to find ways of suspending the audience's tendency to empathize with the characters. Underneath the bizarre surface, the situation of Laura Logan and the others is bleak: their lives are aimless and disappointed; their relationships are external, superficial, and self-defeating; the play expresses the 'anarchic farce' which Mortimer thinks characteristic of modern English life. In performance the object is to make the audience laugh, and to cover over the underlying sense of desperation. 'Comedy', as Mortimer argues in his defence of farce, 'is the only thing worth writing in this despairing world . . . It may be that only in the most secure and optimistic ages can good tragedies be written. Our present situation, stumbling into a misty future filled with uncertainty and mistrust, is far too serious to be described in terms that give us no opportunity to laugh.' In the course of the play's action we are to be caught up in the mechanistic charade of farce, accepting the set conditions of this distanced, abstract world where people are immune to physical or emotional pain, where even love and death involve difficulties which are only technical. For success, the genre must achieve in each member of its audience an anaesthesia of the heart. Clumsily presented, this kind of drama can lapse into offensive bad taste. In a more secure age a still optimistic George Bernard Shaw poured moral abuse on the heartlessness of farce: 'To laugh without sympathy is a ruinous abuse of a noble function; and the degradation of any race may be measured by the degree of their addiction to it . . . the deliberate indulgence of that horrible, derisive joy in humiliation and suffering is the beastliest element in human nature.' Each of the plays in this volume contains some element of comedy, and much of the laughter involves humiliation and suffering; but none of these plays is blighted by the mindlessness or the cruelty which offended Shaw in our theatres in the 1890s. These plays by Edward Albee, Samuel Beckett, Don Haworth, John Mortimer, Harold Pinter, and Tom Stoppard are offered as representative not only of the craftsmanship of our theatrical writing, but also of the human sympathy which characterizes our best plays.

When the last volume in this series was produced (in 1962) it might have been assumed that the one-acter or short play would soon be a vanishing art. The theatre itself no longer has room for 'curtain-raisers' and an evening of linked playlets seems to have little appeal to the general public. It is in this context that radio has carried out an important rescue operation. Television has not had quite the same influence, partly because of the gradual decrease of the single play in favour of the series (*Z Cars, The Likely Lads, Coronation Street*) which are thought to build audiences, but also because television remains primarily a director's medium in which dialogue tends to become obliterated by visual business and a brilliantly developed realism of delivery. Indeed the most striking achievements of television drama, for instance the work of Garnett and Loach (*Cathy Come Home, The Big Flame*) and John Hopkins (*Talking to a Stranger*) would almost disappear if printed between the covers of a book.

Radio, however, remains essentially a writer's medium; it is the words that count, not the ironmongery. It is fortunate, too, to have in Radio 3 a network which still regards the promotion of good new playwrights as an important public duty, however unfavourable the audience's response may be in the first instance. Today there are even more new plays on radio that in the golden forties and fifties and, more important still, the general average of new radio writing is definitely higher than before. Radio writing allows the author an astonishing, indeed frightening, freedom of treatment and location. There is the possibility of cross-cutting, flashback, interior monologue, multi-layered sequences, dreams, narrators, projections of the imagination. The scene can shift quite literally from the North Pole to a Hammersmith dance hall with a few well-chosen lines of dialogue and some simple effects. Flowers and animals can talk, and not infrequently do.

It is not surprising, therefore, that all of the authors in this volume have written for radio (including Albee who recently accepted a commission under an international scheme initiated by the BBC); two of them (Stoppard and Mortimer) started their careers as radio playwrights, while Haworth has scarcely written for any other medium and both Beckett and Pinter have a very special devotion to it.

For whatever medium these plays are written, however, they all have important elements in common: they are not about abstract ideas nor are they mere feats of verbal engineering. They are about human beings, however agonized or absurd the world that these human beings inhabit. They are rooted, therefore, in a reality with which the audience can identify. Through this identification we learn something new, something fresh about ourselves and the world we live in. This resonance is still the hallmark of good playwrighting and is what makes the British theatre still among the most exciting in the world; without it a play, whether it be five minutes or five hours in length, has no hold on our imagination.

JAMES REDMOND
HALLAM TENNYSON

PLAY

Samuel Beckett

Characters

All applications for permission to perform this play must be made in advance to: Spokesmen, 1 Craven Hill, London W2 3EP.

PLAY

*Front centre, touching one another, three identical grey urns
(see page 17) about one yard high. From each a head pro-
trudes, the neck held fast in the urn's mouth. The heads
are those, from left to right as seen from auditorium, of* W2,
M *and* W1. *They face undeviatingly front throughout the
play. Faces so lost to age and aspect as to seem almost part
of urns. But no masks.*

*Their speech is provoked by a spotlight projected on faces
alone. See page 16.*

*The transfer of light from one face to another is immediate.
No blackout, ie return to almost complete darkness of
opening, except where indicated.*

The response to light is immediate.

*Faces impassive throughout. Voices toneless except where an
expression is indicated.*

Rapid tempo throughout.

*The curtain rises on a stage in almost complete darkness. Urns
just discernible. Five seconds.*

*Faint spots simultaneously on three faces. Three seconds.
Voices faint, largely unintelligible.*

W1 — *Together. See page 16* — Yes, strange, darkness best, and the darker
the worse, till all dark, then all well, for
the time, but it will come, the time will
come, the thing is there, you'll see it, get
off me, keep off me, all dark, all still, all
over, wiped out—

W2 — Yes, perhaps, a shade gone, I suppose,
some might say, poor thing, a shade gone,
just a shade, in the head—(*faint wild
laugh*)—just a shade, but I doubt it, *I*
doubt it, not really, I'm all right, still all
right, do my best, all I can—

M — Yes, peace, one assumed, all out, all the
pain, all as if . . . never been, it will come

)   —(*hiccup*)—pardon, no sense in this, oh
)   I know . . . none the less, one assumed,
)   peace . . . I mean . . . not merely all over,
)   but as if . . . never been—

Spots off. Blackout. Five seconds. Strong spots simultaneously on three faces. Three seconds. Voices normal strength.

w1)   ⌠ I said to him, Give her up—
w2 } *Together.* ⟨ One morning as I was sitting—
m)   ⌡ We were not long together—

Spots off. Blackout. Five seconds. Spot on w1.

w1: I said to him, Give her up. I swore by all I held most sacred—

Spot from w1 to w2.

w2: One morning as I was sitting stitching by the open window she burst in and flew at me. Give him up, she screamed, he's mine. Her photographs were kind to her. Seeing her now for the first time full length in the flesh I understood why he preferred me.

Spot from w2 to m.

m: We were not long together when she smelled the rat. Give up that whore, she said, or I'll cut my throat— (*hiccup*) pardon—so help me God. I knew she could have no proof. So I told her I did not know what she was talking about.

Spot from m to w2.

w2: What are you talking about? I said, stitching away. Someone yours? Give up whom? I smell you off him, she screamed, he stinks of bitch.

Spot from w2 to w1.

w1: Though I had him dogged for months by a first-rate man, no shadow of proof was forthcoming. And there was no denying that he continued as . . . assiduous as ever. This, and his horror of the merely Platonic thing, made me

sometimes wonder if I were not accusing him unjustly. Yes.
Spot from W1 *to* M.

M: What have you to complain of? I said. Have I been neglecting you? How could we be together in the way we are if there were someone else? Loving her as I did, with all my heart, I could not but feel sorry for her.
Spot from M *to* W2.

W2: Fearing she was about to offer me violence I rang for Erskine and had her shown out. Her parting words, as he could testify, if he is still living, and has not forgotten, coming and going on the earth, letting people in, showing people out, were to the effect that she would settle my hash. I confess this did alarm me a little, at the time.
Spot from W2 *to* M.

M: She was not convinced. I might have known. I smell her off you, she kept saying. There was no answer to this. So I took her in my arms and swore I could not live without her. I meant it, what is more. Yes, I am sure I did. She did not repulse me.
Spot from M *to* W1.

W1: Judge then of my astoundment when one fine morning, as I was sitting stricken in the morning room, he slunk in, fell on his knees before me, buried his face in my lap and . . . confessed.
Spot from W1 *to* M.

M: She put a bloodhound on me, but I had a little chat with him. He was glad of the extra money.
Spot from M *to* W2.

W2: Why don't you get out, I said, when he started moaning about his home life, there is obviously nothing between you any more. Or is there?
Spot from W2 *to* W1.

W1: I confess my first feeling was one of wonderment. What a male!
Spot from W1 *to* M. *He opens his mouth to speak. Spot from* M *to* W2.

W2: Anything between us, he said, what do you take me for,

a something machine? And of course with him no danger of the . . . spiritual thing. Then why don't you get out? I said. I sometimes wondered if he was not living with her for her money.

    Spot from W2 *to* M.

M: The next thing was the scene between them. I can't have her crashing in here, she said, threatening to take my life. I must have looked incredulous. Ask Erskine, she said, if you don't believe me. But she threatens to take her own, I said. Not yours? she said. No, I said, hers. We had fun trying to work this out.

    Spot from M *to* W1.

W1: Then I forgave him. To what will love not stoop! I suggested a little jaunt to celebrate, to the Riviera or our darling Grand Canary. He was looking pale. Peaked. But this was not possible just then. Professional commitments.

    Spot from W1 *to* W2.

W2: She came again. Just strolled in. All honey. Licking her lips. Poor thing. I was doing my nails, by the open window. He has told me all about it, she said. Who he, I said filing away, and what it? I know what torture you must be going through, she said, and I have dropped in to say I bear you no ill-feeling. I rang for Erskine.

    Spot from W2 *to* M.

M: Then I got frightened and made a clean breast of it. She was looking more and more desperate. She had a razor in her vanity-bag. Adulterers, take warning, never admit.

    Spot from M *to* W1.

W1: When I was satisfied it was all over I went to have a gloat. Just a common tart. What he could have found in her when he had me—

    Spot from W1 *to* W2.

W2: When he came again we had it out. I felt like death. He went on about why he had to tell her. Too risky and so on. That meant he had gone back to her. Back to that!

    Spot from W2 *to* W1.

W1: Pudding face, puffy, spots, blubber mouth, jowls, no

neck, dugs you could—
>*Spot from* W1 *to* W2.

W2: He went on and on. I could hear a mower. An old hand mower. I stopped him and said that whatever I might feel I had no silly threats to offer—but not much stomach for her leavings either. He thought that over for a bit.
>*Spot from* W2 *to* W1.

W1: Calves like a flunkey—
>*Spot from* W1 *to* M.

M: When I saw her again she knew. She was looking— (*hiccup*)—wretched. Pardon. Some fool was cutting grass. A little rush, then another. The problem was how to convince her that no . . . revival of intimacy was involved. I couldn't. I might have known. So I took her in my arms and said I could not go on living without her. I don't believe I could have.
>*Spot from* M *to* W2.

W2: The only solution was to go away together. He swore we should as soon as he had put his affairs in order. In the meantime we were to carry on as before. By that he meant as best we could.
>*Spot from* W2 *to* W1.

W1: So he was mine again. All mine. I was happy again. I went about singing. The world—
>*Spot from* W1 *to* M.

M: At home all heart to heart, new leaf and bygones bygones. I ran into your ex-doxy, she said one night, on the pillow, you're well out of that. Rather uncalled for, I thought. I am indeed, sweetheart, I said, I am indeed. God what vermin women. Thanks to you, angel, I said.
>*Spot from* M *to* W1.

W1: Then I began to smell her off him again. Yes.
>*Spot from* W1 *to* W2.

W2: When he stopped coming I was prepared. More or less.
>*Spot from* W2 *to* M.

M: Finally it was all too much. I simply could no longer—

Spot from M *to* W1.

W1: Before I could do anything he disappeared. That meant she had won. That slut! I couldn't credit it. I lay stricken for weeks. Then I drove over to her place. It was all bolted and barred. All grey with frozen dew. On the way back by Ash and Snodland—

Spot from W1 *to* M.

M: I simply could no longer—

Spot from M *to* W2.

W2: I made a bundle of things and burnt them. It was November and the bonfire was going. All night I smelt them smouldering.

Spot off W2. *Blackout. Five seconds. Spots half previous strength simultaneously on three faces. Three seconds. Voices proportionately lower.*

W1 ⎫
W2 ⎬ *Together.* ⎧ Mercy, mercy—
M   ⎭   ⎨ To say I am—
               ⎩ When first this change—

Spots off. Blackout. Five seconds. Spot on M.

M: When first this change I actually thanked God. I thought, It is done, it is said, now all is going out—

Spot from M *to* W1.

W1: Mercy, mercy, tongue still hanging out for mercy. It will come. You haven't seen me. But you will. Then it will come.

Spot from W1 *to* W2.

W2: To say I am not disappointed, no, I am. I had anticipated something better. More restful.

Spot from W2 *to* W1.

W1: Or you will weary of me. Get off me.

Spot from W1 *to* M.

M: Down, all going down, into the dark, peace is coming, I thought, after all, at last, I was right, after all, thank God, when first this change.

Spot from M *to* W2.

W2: Less confused. Less confusing. At the same time I prefer this to . . . the other thing. Definitely. There are endurable moments.

Spot from W2 *to* M.

M: I thought.

Spot from M *to* W2.

W2: When you go out—and I go out. Some day you will tire of me and go out . . . for good.

Spot from W2 *to* W1.

W1: Hellish half-light.

Spot from W1 *to* M.

M: Peace, yes, I suppose, a kind of peace, and all that pain as if . . . never been.

Spot from M *to* W2.

W2: Give me up, as a bad job. Go away and start poking and pecking at someone else. On the other hand—

Spot from W2 *to* W1.

W1: Get off me! (*Vehement*) Get off me!

Spot from W1 *to* M.

M: It will come. Must come. There is no future in this.

Spot from M *to* W2.

W2: On the other hand things may disimprove, there is that danger.

Spot from W2 *to* M.

M: Oh of course I know now—

Spot from M *to* W1.

W1: Is it that I do not tell the truth, is that it, that some day somehow I may tell the truth at last and then no more light light at last, for the truth?

Spot from W1 *to* W2.

W2: You might get angry and blaze me clean out of my wits. Mightn't you?

Spot from W2 *to* M.

M: I know now, all that was just . . . play. And all this? When will all this—

Spot from M *to* W1.

w1: Is that it?
  Spot from w1 *to* w2.
w2: Mightn't you?
  Spot from w2 *to* M.
M: All this, when will all this have been . . . just play?
  Spot from M *to* w1.
w1: I can do nothing . . . for anybody . . . any more . . .
  thank God. So it must be something I have to say. How the
  mind works still!
  Spot from w1 *to* w2.
w2: But I doubt it. It would not be like you somehow. And
  you must know I am doing my best. Or don't you?
  Spot from w2 *to* M.
M: Perhaps they have become friends. Perhaps sorrow—
  Spot from M *to* w1.
w1: But I have said all I can. All you let me. All I—
  Spot from w1 *to* M.
M: Perhaps sorrow has brought them together.
  Spot from M *to* w2.
w2: No doubt I make the same mistake as when it was the
  sun that shone, of looking for sense where possibly there is
  none.
  Spot from w2 *to* M.
M: Perhaps they meet, and sit, over a cup of that green tea
  they both so loved, without · milk or sugar, not even a
  squeeze of lemon—
  Spot from M *to* w2.
w2: Are you listening to me? Is anyone listening to me?
  Is anyone looking at me? Is anyone bothering about me at
  all?
  Spot from w2 *to* M.
M: Not even a squeeze of—
  Spot from M *to* w1.
w1: Is it something I should do with my face, other than
  utter? Weep?
  Spot from w1 *to* w2.
w2: Am I taboo, I wonder. Not necessarily, now that all

danger is averted. That poor creature—I can hear her—that poor creature—

Spot from W2 *to* W1.

W1: Bite off my tongue and swallow it? Spit it out? Would that placate you? How the mind works still to be sure!

Spot from W1 *to* M.

M: Meet, and sit, now in the one dear old place, now in the other, and sorrow together, and compare—(*hiccup*) pardon —happy memories.

Spot from M *to* W1.

W1: If only I could think. There is no sense in this . . . either, none whatsoever. I can't.

Spot from W1 *to* W2.

W2: That poor creature who tried to seduce you, what ever became of her, do you suppose?—I can hear her. Poor thing.

Spot from W2 *to* M.

M: Personally I always preferred Lipton's.

Spot from M *to* W1.

W1: And that all is falling, all fallen, from the beginning, on empty air. Nothing being asked at all. No one asking me for anything at all.

Spot from W1 *to* W2.

W2: They might even feel sorry for me, if they could see me. But never so sorry as I for them.

Spot from W2 *to* W1.

W1: I can't.

Spot from W1 *to* W2.

W2: Kissing their sour kisses.

Spot from W2 *to* M.

M: I pity them in any case, yes, compare my lot with theirs, however blessed, and—

Spot from M *to* W1.

W1: I can't. The mind won't have it. It would have to go. Yes.

Spot from W1 *to* M.

M: Pity them.

Spot from M *to* W2.

W2: What do you do when you go out? Sift?

Spot from W2 *to* M.

M: Am I hiding something? Have I lost—

Spot from M *to* W1.

W1: She had means, I fancy, though she lived like a pig.

Spot from W1 *to* W2.

W2: Like dragging a great roller, on a scorching day. The
strain . . . to get it moving, momentum coming—

Spot off W2. *Blackout. Three seconds. Spot on* W2.

W2: Kill it and strain again.

Spot from W2 *to* M.

M: Have I lost . . .the thing you want? Why go out? Why
go—

Spot from M *to* W2.

W2: And you perhaps pitying me, thinking, Poor thing
needs a rest.

Spot from W2 *to* W1.

W1: Perhaps she has taken him away to live . . . somewhere in
the sun.

Spot from W1 *to* M.

M: Why go down? Why not—

Spot from M *to* W2.

W2: I don't know.

Spot from W2 *to* W1.

W1: Perhaps she is sitting somewhere, by the open window,
her hands folded in her lap, gazing down out over the
olives—

Spot from W1 *to* M.

M: Why not keep on glaring at me without ceasing? I
might start to rave and—(*hiccup*)—bring it up for you.
Par—

Spot from M *to* W2.

W2: No.

Spot from W2 *to* M.

M: —don.

Spot from M *to* W1.

w1: Gazing down out over the olives, then the sea, wondering what can be keeping him, growing cold. Shadow stealing over everything. Creeping. Yes.

Spot from w1 *to* M.

M: To think we were never together.

Spot from M *to* w2.

w2: Am I not perhaps a little unhinged already?

Spot from w2 *to* w1.

w1: Poor creature. Poor creatures.

Spot from w1 *to* M.

M: Never woke together, on a May morning, the first to wake to wake the other two. Then in a little dinghy—

Spot from M *to* w1.

w1: Penitence, yes, at a pinch, atonement, one was resigned, but no, that does not seem to be the point either.

Spot from w1 *to* w2.

w2: I say, am I not perhaps a little unhinged already? (*Hopefully*) Just a little? (*Pause*) I doubt it.

Spot from w2 *to* M.

M: A little dinghy—

Spot from M *to* w1.

w1: Silence and darkness were all I craved. Well, I get a certain amount of both. They being one. Perhaps it is more wickedness to pray for more.

Spot from w1 *to* M.

M: A little dinghy, on the river, I resting on my oars, they lolling on air-pillows in the stern . . . sheets. Drifting. Such fantasies.

Spot from M *to* w1.

w1: Hellish half-light.

Spot from w1 *to* w2.

w2: A shade gone. In the head. Just a shade. I doubt it.

Spot from w2 *to* M.

M: We were not civilized.

Spot from M *to* w1.

w1: Dying for dark—and the darker the worse. Strange.

Spot from w1 *to* M.

M: Such fantasies. Then. And now—
   Spot from M *to* W2.
W1: *I* doubt it.
   Pause. Peal of wild low laughter from W2 *cut short as spot from her to* W1.
W1: Yes, and the whole thing there, all there, staring you in the face. You'll see it. Get off me. Or weary.
   Spot from W1 *to* M.
M: And now, that you are . . . mere eye. Just looking. At my face. On and off.
   Spot from M *to* W1.
W1: Weary of playing with me. Get off me. Yes.
   Spot from W1 *to* M.
M: Looking for something. In my face. Some truth. In my eyes. Not even.
   Spot from M *to* W2. *Laugh as before from* W2 *cut short as spot from her to* M.
M: Mere eye. No mind. Opening and shutting on me. Am I as much—
   Spot off M. *Blackout. Three seconds. Spot on* M.
M: Am I as much as . . . being seen?

   Spot off M. *Blackout. Five seconds. Faint spots simultaneously on three faces. Three seconds. Voices faint, largely unintelligible.*

W1 ⎫
W2 ⎬ *Together.* ⎰ Yes, strange, etc.
M ⎭   ⎱ Yes, perhaps, etc.
              Yes, peace, etc.

   Repeat play.

M (*closing repeat*): Am I as much as . . . being seen?
   Spot off M. *Blackout. Five seconds. Strong spots simultaneously on three faces. Three seconds. Voices normal strength.*

W1 ⎫
W2 ⎬ *Together.* ⎰ I said to him, Give her up—
M ⎭   ⎨ One morning as I was sitting
                   ⎩ We were not long together—

   Spots off Blackout. Five seconds. Spot on M.
M: We were not long together—
   Spot off M. *Blackout. Five seconds.*

CURTAIN

LIGHT

The source of light is single and must not be situated outside the ideal space (stage) occupied by its victims.

The optimum position for the spot is at the centre of the footlights, the faces being thus lit at close quarters and from below.

When exceptionally three spots are required to light the three faces simultaneously, they should be as a single spot branching into three.

Apart from these moments a single mobile spot should be used, swivelling at maximum speed from one face to another as required.

The method consisting in assigning to each face a separate fixed spot is unsatisfactory in that it is less expressive of a unique inquisitor than the single mobile spot.

CHORUS

W1	Yes strange	darkness best	and the darker	the worse
W2	Yes perhaps	a shade gone	I suppose	some might say
M	Yes peace	one assumed	all out	all the pain
W1	till all dark	then all well	for the time	but it will come
W2	poor thing	a shade gone	just a shade	in the head
M	all as if	never been	it will come	(*hiccup*) pardon
W1	the time will come		the thing is there	you'll see it
W2	(*laugh* - - - - - - - - -)		just a shade	but I doubt it
M	no sense in this		oh I know	none the less
W1	get off me	keep off me	all dark	all still
W2	*I* doubt it	not really	I'm all right	still all right
M	one assumed	peace I mean	not merely	all over
W1	all over	wiped out—		
W2	do my best	all I can—		
M	but as if	never been—		

URNS

In order for the urns to be only one yard high, it is necessary either that traps be used, enabling the actors to stand below stage level, or that they kneel throughout play, the urns being open at the back.

Should traps be not available, and the kneeling posture found impracticable, the actors should stand, the urns be enlarged to full length and moved back from front to mid-stage, the tallest actor setting the height, the broadest the breadth, to which the three urns should conform.

The sitting posture results in urns of unacceptable bulk and is not to be considered.

REPEAT

The repeat may be an exact replica of first statement or it may present an element of variation.

In other words, the light may operate the second time exactly as it did the first (exact replica) or it may try a different method (variation).

The London production (and in a lesser degree the Paris production) opted for the variation with following deviations from first statement:

1. Introduction of an abridged chorus, cut short on laugh of W2, to open fragment of second repeat.

2. Light less strong in repeat and voices corespondingly lower, giving the following schema, where A is the highest level of light and voice and E the lowest:

C First chorus.
A First part of 1. } 1
B Second part of 1.

D Second chorus.
B First part of Repeat 1. } Repeat 1
C Second part of Repeat 1.

E Abridged chorus.
C Fragment of Repeat 2 } Fragment of Repeat 2

3. Breathless quality in voices from beginning of Repeat 1 and increasing to end of play.

4. Changed order of speeches in repeat as far as this is compatible with unchanged continuity for actors. Eg the order of interrogation W1, W2, M, W2, W1, M at opening of 1 becomes W2, W1, M, W2, M, W1 at opening of repeat, and so on if and as desired.

Characters

PETER: A man in his early forties, neither fat nor gaunt, neither handsome nor homely. He wears tweeds, smokes a pipe, carries horn-rimmed glasses. Although he is moving into middle age, his dress and his manner would suggest a man younger.

JERRY: A man in his late thirties, not poorly dressed, but carelessly. What was once a trim and lightly muscled body has begun to go to fat; and while he is no longer handsome, it is evident that he once was. His fall from physical grace should not suggest debauchery; he has, to come closest to it, a great weariness.

THE ZOO STORY

It is Central Park; a Sunday afternoon in summer; the present. There are two park benches, one towards either side of the stage; they both face the audience. Behind them: foliage, trees, sky. At the beginning, PETER *is seated on one of the benches.*

As the curtain rises, PETER *is seated on the bench stage-right. He is reading a book. He stops reading, cleans his glasses, goes back to reading.* JERRY *enters.*

JERRY: I've been to the zoo. (PETER *doesn't notice*) I said, I've been to the zoo. MISTER, I'VE BEEN TO THE ZOO!

PETER: Hm? . . . What? . . . I'm sorry, were you talking to me?

JERRY: I went to the zoo, and then I walked until I came here. Have I been walking north?

PETER (*puzzled*): North? Why . . . I . . . I think so. Let me see.

JERRY (*pointing past the audience*): Is that Fifth Avenue?

PETER: Why yes; yes, it is.

JERRY: And what is that cross street there; that one, to the right?

PETER: That? Oh, that's Seventy-fourth Street.

JERRY: And the zoo is around Sixty-fifth Street; so, I've been walking north.

PETER (*anxious to get back to his reading*): Yes: it would seem so.

JERRY: Good old north.

PETER (*lightly, by reflex*): Ha, ha.

JERRY (*after a slight pause*): But not due north.

PETER: I . . . well, no, not due north; but, we . . . call it north. It's northerly.

JERRY (*watches as* PETER, *anxious to dismiss him, prepares his pipe*): Well, boy; *you're* not going to get lung cancer, are you?

PETER (*looks up, a little annoyed, then smiles*): No, sir. Not from this.

JERRY: No, sir. What you'll probably get is cancer of the mouth, and then you'll have to wear one of those things Freud wore after they took one whole side of his jaw away. What do they call those things?

PETER (*uncomfortable*): A prosthesis?

JERRY: The very thing! A prosthesis. You're an educated man, aren't you? Are you a doctor?

PETER: Oh, no; no. I read about it somewhere: *Time* magazine, I think. (*He turns to his book*)

JERRY: Well, *Time* magazine isn't for blockheads.

PETER: No, I suppose not.

JERRY (*after a pause*): Boy, I'm glad that's Fifth Avenue there.

PETER (*vaguely*): Yes.

JERRY: I don't like the west side of the park much.

PETER: Oh? (*then, slightly wary, but interested*) Why?

JERRY (*off-hand*): I don't know.

PETER: Oh. (*He returns to his book*)

JERRY (*stands for a few seconds, looking at* PETER, *who finally looks up again, puzzled*): Do you mind if we talk?

PETER (*obviously minding*): Why . . . no, no.

JERRY: Yes you do; you do.

PETER (*puts his book down, his pipe out and away, smiling*): No, really; I don't mind.

JERRY: Yes you do.

PETER (*finally decided*): No; I don't mind at all, really.

JERRY: It's . . . it's a nice day.

PETER (*stares unnecessarily at the sky*): Yes. Yes, it is; lovely.

JERRY: I've been to the zoo.

PETER: Yes, I think you said so . . . didn't you?

JERRY: You'll read about it in the papers tomorrow, if you don't see it on your TV tonight. You have TV, haven't you?

PETER: Why yes, we have two; one for the children.

JERRY: You're married!

PETER (*with pleased emphasis*): Why, certainly.

JERRY: It isn't a law, for God's sake.

PETER: No . . . no, of course not.

JERRY: And you have a wife.

PETER (*bewildered by the seeming lack of communication*): Yes!

JERRY: And you have children.

PETER: Yes; two.

JERRY: Boys?

PETER: No, girls . . . both girls.

JERRY: But you wanted boys.

PETER: Well . . . naturally, every man wants a son, but . . .

JERRY (*lightly mocking*): But that's the way the cookie crumbles?

PETER (*annoyed*): I wasn't going to say that.

JERRY: And you're not going to have any more kids, are you?

PETER (*a bit distantly*): No. No more. (*Then back, and irksome*) Why did you say that? How would you know about that?

JERRY: The way you cross your legs, perhaps; something in the voice. Or maybe I'm just guessing. Is it your wife?

PETER (*furious*): That's none of your business! (*A silence*) Do you understand?

(JERRY *nods.* PETER *is quiet now*)

Well, you're right. We'll have no more children.

JERRY (*softly*): That *is* the way the cookie crumbles.

PETER (*forgiving*): Yes . . . I guess so.

JERRY: Well, now; what else?

PETER: What were you saying about the zoo . . . that I'd read about it, or see . . .?

JERRY: I'll tell you about it, soon. Do you mind if I ask you questions?

PETER: Oh, not really.

JERRY: I'll tell you why I do it; I don't talk to many people— except to say like: give me a beer, or where's the john, or what time does the feature go on, or keep your hands to yourself, buddy. You know—things like that.

PETER: I must say I don't . . .

JERRY: But every once in a while I like to talk to somebody, really *talk*; like to get to know somebody, know all about him.

PETER (*lightly laughing, still a little uncomfortable*): And am I the guinea pig for today?

JERRY: On a sun-drenched Sunday afternoon like this: Who better than a nice married man with two daughters and . . . uh . . . a dog?

(PETER *shakes his head*)

No? Two dogs.

(PETER *shakes his head again*)

Hm. No dogs?

(PETER *shakes his head, sadly*)

Oh, that's a shame. But you look like an animal man. CATS?

(PETER *nods his head, ruefully*)

Cats! But, that can't be your idea. No, sir. Your wife and daughters?

(PETER *nods his head*)

Is there anything else I should know?

PETER (*has to clear his throat*): There are . . . there are two parakeets. One . . . uh . . . one for each of my daughters.

JERRY: Birds.

PETER: My daughters keep them in a cage in their bedroom.

JERRY: Do they carry disease? The birds.

PETER: I don't believe so.

JERRY: That's too bad. If they did you could set them loose in the house and the cats could eat them and die, maybe.

(PETER *looks blank for a moment, then laughs*)

And what else? What do you do to support your enormous household?

PETER: I . . . uh . . . I have an executive position with a . . . a small publishing house. We . . . uh . . . we publish text-books.

JERRY: That sounds nice; very nice. What do you make?

PETER (*still cheerful*): Now look here!

JERRY: Oh, come on.

PETER: Well, I make around eighteen thousand a year, but I don't carry more than forty dollars at any one time . . . in case you're a . . . a holdup man . . . ha, ha, ha.

JERRY (*ignoring the above*): Where do you live?

(PETER *is reluctant*)

Oh, look; I'm not going to rob you, and I'm not going to kidnap your parakeets, your cats or your daughters.

PETER (*too loud*): I live between Lexington and Third Avenue, on Seventy-fourth Street.

JERRY: That wasn't so hard, was it?

PETER: I didn't mean to seem . . . ah . . . it's just that you don't really carry on a conversation; you just ask questions. And I'm . . . I'm normally . . . uh . . . reticent. Why do you just stand there?

JERRY: I'll start walking around in a little while, and eventually I'll sit down. (*Recalling*) Wait until you see the expression on his face.

PETER: What? Whose face? Look here? is this something about the zoo?

JERRY (*distantly*): The what?

PETER: The zoo; the zoo. Something about the zoo.

JERRY: The zoo?

PETER: You've mentioned it several times.

JERRY (*still distant, but returning abruptly*): The zoo? Oh, yes; the zoo. I was there before I came here. I told you that. Say, what's the dividing line between upper-middle-middle-class and lower-upper-middle-class?

PETER: My dear fellow, I . . .

JERRY: Don't my dear fellow me.

PETER (*unhappily*): Was I patronizing? I believe I was; I'm sorry. But, you see, your question about the classes bewildered me.

JERRY: And when you're bewildered you become patronizing?

PETER: I . . . I don't express myself too well, sometimes. (*He attempts a joke on himself*) I'm in publishing, not writing.

JERRY (*amused, but not at the humour*): So be it. The truth *is*: *I* was being patronizing.

PETER: Oh, now; you needn't say that.

(*It is at this point that* JERRY *may begin to move about the stage with slowly increasing determination and authority, but pacing himself, so that the long speech about the dog comes at the high point of the arc.*)

JERRY: All right. Who are your favourite writers? Baudelaire and J.P. Marquand?

PETER (*wary*): Well, I like a great many writers; I have a considerable . . . catholicity of taste, if I may say so. Those two men are fine, each in his way. (*Warming up*) Baudelaire, of course . . . uh . . . is by far the finer of the two, but Marquand has a place . . . in our . . . uh . . . national . . .

JERRY: Skip it.

PETER: I . . . sorry.

JERRY: Do you know what I did before I went to the zoo today? I walked all the way up Fifth Avenue from Washington Square; all the way.

PETER: Oh; you live in the Village! (*This seems to enlighten Peter*)

JERRY: No, I don't. I took the subway down to the Village so I could walk all the way up Fifth Avenue to the zoo. It's one of those things a person has to do; <u>sometimes a person has to go a very long distance out of his way to come back a short distance correctly.</u>

PETER (*almost pouting*): Oh, I thought you lived in the Village.

JERRY: What were you trying to do? Make sense out of things? Bring order? The old pigeonhole bit? Well, that's easy; I'll tell you. I live in a four-storey brownstone rooming-house on the upper West Side between Columbus Avenue and Central Park West. I live on the top floor; rear; west. It's a laughably small room, and one of my walls is made of beaverboard; this beaverboard separates my room from another laughably small room, so I assume that the two rooms were once one room, a small room, but not necessarily laughable. The room beyond my beaverboard wall is occupied by a coloured queen who always keeps his door open; well, not always but *always* when he's plucking his eyebrows, which he does with Buddhist concentration. This coloured queen has rotten teeth, which is rare, and he has a Japanese kimono, which is also pretty rare; and he wears this kimono to and from the john in the hall, which is pretty frequent. I mean, he goes to the john a lot. He never bothers me, and never brings anyone up to his room. All he does is pluck his eyebrows, wear his kimono and go to the john. Now, the two front rooms on my floor are a little larger, I guess; but they're pretty small, too. There's a Puerto Rican family in one of them, a husband, a wife, and some kids; I don't know how many. These people entertain a lot. And in the other front room, there's somebody living there, but I don't know who it is. I've never seen who it is. Never. Never ever.

PETER (*embarrassed*): Why . . . why do you live there?

JERRY (*from a distance again*): I don't know.

PETER: It doesn't sound a very nice place . . . where you live.

JERRY: Well, no; it isn't an apartment in the East Seventies.

But, then again, I don't have one wife, two daughters, two cats and two parakeets. What I do have, I have toilet articles, a few clothes, a hot plate that I'm not supposed to have, a can opener, one that works with a key, you know: a knife, two forks, and two spoons, one small, one large; three plates, a cup, a saucer, a drinking glass, two picture frames, both empty, eight or nine books, a pack of pornographic playing-cards, regular deck, an old Western Union typewriter that prints nothing but capital letters, and a small strong-box without a lock which has in it . . . what? Rocks! Some rocks . . . sea-rounded rocks I picked up on the beach when I was a kid. Under which . . . weighed down . . . are some letters . . . please letters . . . please why don't you do this, and please when will you do that letters. And when letters, too. When will you write? When will you come? When? These letters are from more recent years.

PETER (*stares glumly at his shoes, then—*): About those two empty picture frames . . .?

JERRY: I don't see why they need any explanation at all. Isn't it clear? I don't have pictures of anyone to put in them.

PETER: Your parents . . . perhaps . . . a girl-friend . . .

JERRY: You're a very sweet man; and you're possessed of a truly enviable innocence. But good old Mom and good old Pop are dead . . . you know? . . . I'm broken up about it, too . . . I mean really. BUT. That particular vaudeville act is playing the cloud circuit now, so I don't see how I can look at them, all neat and framed. Besides, or, rather, to be pointed about it, good old Mom walked out on good old Pop when I was ten and a half years old; she embarked on an adulterous turn of our southern states . . . a journey of a year's duration . . . and her most constant companion . . . among others, among many others . . . was a Mr Barleycorn. At least, that's what good old Pop told me after he went down . . . came back . . . brought her body north. We'd received the news between Christmas and New Year's, you see, that good old Mom had parted with the

ghost in some dump in Alabama. And, without the ghost
. . . she was less welcome. I mean, what was she? A stiff . . .
a northern stiff. At any rate, good old Pop celebrated the
New Year for an even two weeks and then slapped into the
front of a somewhat moving city omnibus, which sort of
cleaned things out family-wise. Well no; then there was
Mom's sister, who was given neither to sin nor the con-
solations of the bottle. I moved in on her, and my memory
of her is slight excepting I remember still that she did all
things dourly: sleeping, eating, working, praying. She
dropped dead on the stairs to her apartment, my apartment
then, too, on the afternoon of my high school graduation.
A terribly middle-European joke, if you ask me.

PETER: Oh, my; oh, my.

JERRY: Oh, your what? But that was a long time ago, and I
have no feeling about any of it that I care to admit to myself. Perhaps you can see, though, why good old Mom and
good old Pop are frameless. What's your name? Your
first name?

PETER: I'm Peter.

JERRY: I'd forgotten to ask you. I'm Jerry.

PETER (*with a slight nervous laugh*): Hello, Jerry.

JERRY (*nods his hello*): And let's see now; what's the point of
having a girl's picture, especially in two frames? I have two
picture frames, you remember. I never see the pretty little
ladies more than once, and most of them wouldn't be
caught in the same room with a camera. It's odd, and I
wonder if it's sad.

PETER: The girls?

JERRY: No. I wonder if it's sad that I never see the little ladies
more than once. I've never been able to have sex with, or
how is it put? . . . make love to anybody more than once.
Once; that's it . . . Oh, wait; for a week and a half, when I
was fifteen . . . and I hang my head in shame that puberty
was late . . . I was a h-o-m-o-s-e-x-u-a-l. I mean, I was
queer . . . (*Very fast*) . . . queer, queer, queer . . . with
bells ringing, banners snapping in the wind. And for those

eleven days, I met at least twice a day with the park super-
intendent's son . . . a Greek boy, whose birthday was the
same as mine, except he was a year older. I think I was very
much in love . . . maybe just with sex. But that was the
jazz of a very special hotel, wasn't it? And now; oh, I do
love the little ladies; really, I love them. For about an
hour.

PETER: Well, it seems perfectly simple to me . . .

JERRY (*angry*): Look! Are you going to tell me to get married
and have parakeets!

PETER (*angry himself*): Forget the parakeets! And stay single
if you want to. It's no business of mine. I didn't start this
conversation in the . . .

JERRY: All right, all right. I'm sorry. All right? You're not
angry?

PETER (*laughing*): No, I'm not angry.

JERRY (*relieved*): Good. (*Now back to his previous tone*) Interesting that you asked me about the picture frames. I would
have thought that you would have asked me about the
pornographic playing-cards.

PETER (*with a knowing smile*): Oh, I've seen those cards.

JERRY: That's not the point. (*Laughs*) I suppose when you
were a kid you and your pals passed them around, or you
had a pack of your own.

PETER: Well, I guess a lot of us did.

JERRY: And you threw them away just before you got married.

PETER: Oh, now; look here. I didn't *need* anything like that
when I got older.

JERRY: No?

PETER (*embarrassed*): I'd rather not talk about these things.

JERRY: So? Don't. Besides, I wasn't trying to plumb your post-
adolescent sexual life and hard times; what I wanted to get
at is the value difference between pornographic playing-
cards when you're a kid, and pornographic playing-cards
when you're older. It's that when you're a kid you use the
cards as a substitute for a real experience, and when you're
older you use real experience as a substitute for the fantasy.

But I imagine you'd rather hear about what happened at the zoo.

PETER (*enthusiastic*): Oh, yes; the zoo. (*Then awkward*) That is . . . if you . . .

JERRY: Let me tell you about why I went . . . well, let me tell you some things. I've told you about the fourth floor of the rooming-house where I live. I think the rooms are better as you go down, floor by floor. I guess they are; I don't know. I don't know any of the people on the third and second floors. Oh, wait! I do know that there's a lady living on the third floor, in the front. I know because she cries all the time. Whenever I go out or come back in, whenever I pass her door, I always hear her crying, muffled, but . . . very determined. Very determined indeed. But the one I'm getting to, and all about the dog, is the landlady. I don't like to use words that are too harsh in describing people. I don't like to. But the landlady is a fat, ugly, mean, stupid, unwashed, misanthropic, cheap, drunken bag of garbage. And you may have noticed that I very seldom use profanity, so I can't describe her as well as I might.

PETER: You describe her . . . vividly.

JERRY: Well, thanks. Anyway, she has a dog, and I will tell you about the dog, and she and her dog are the gate-keepers of my dwelling. The woman is bad enough; she leans around in the entrance hall, spying to see that I don't bring in things or people, and when she's had her mid-afternoon pint of lemon-flavoured gin she always stops me in the hall, and grabs ahold of my coat or my arm, and she presses her disgusting body up against me to keep me in a corner so she can talk to me. The smell of her body and her breath . . . you can't imagine it . . . and somewhere, somewhere in the back of that pea-sized brain of hers, an organ developed just enough to let her eat, drink and emit, she has some foul parody of sexual desire. And I, Peter, I am the object of her sweaty lust.

PETER: That's disgusting. That's . . . horrible.

JERRY: But I have found a way to keep her off. When she talks to me, when she presses herself to my body and mumbles about her room and how I should come there, I merely say: but, Love; wasn't yesterday enough for you, and the day before? Then she puzzles, she makes slits of her tiny eyes, she sways a little, and then, Peter . . . and it is at this moment that I think I might be doing some good in that tormented house . . . a simple-minded smile begins to form on her unthinkable face, and she giggles and groans as she thinks about yesterday and the day before; as she believes and relives what never happened. Then, she motions to that black monster of a dog she has, and she goes back to her room. And I am safe until our next meeting.

PETER: It's so . . . unthinkable. I find it hard to believe that people such as that really *are*.

JERRY (*lightly mocking*): It's for reading about, isn't it?

PETER (*seriously*): Yes.

JERRY: And fact is better left to fiction. You're right, Peter. Well, what I have been meaning to tell you about is the dog; I shall, now.

PETER (*nervously*): Oh, yes; the dog.

JERRY: Don't go. You're not thinking of going, are you?

PETER: Well . . . no, I don't think so.

JERRY (*as if to a child*): Because after I tell you about the dog, do you know what then? Then . . . then I'll tell you about what happened at the zoo.

PETER (*laughing faintly*): You're . . . you're full of stories, aren't you?

JERRY: You don't *have* to listen. Nobody is holding you here; remember that. Keep that in your mind.

PETER (*irritably*): I know that.

JERRY: You do? Good.

(*The following long speech, it seems to me, should be done with a great deal of action, to achieve a hypnotic effect on Peter, and on the audience too. Some specific actions have been suggested, but the director and the actor playing Jerry might best work it out for themselves.*)

ALL RIGHT: (*As if reading from a huge bill-board*) THE STORY OF JERRY AND THE DOG! (*Natural again*) What I am going to tell you has something to do with how sometimes it's necessary to go a long distance out of the way in order to come back a short distance correctly; or, maybe I only think that it has something to do with that. But, it's why I went to the zoo today, and why I walked north . . . northerly, rather . . . until I came here. All right. The dog, I think I told you, is a black monster of a beast: an over-sized head, tiny, tiny ears, and eyes . . . bloodshot, infected, maybe; and a body you can see the ribs through the skin. The dog is black, all black; all black except for the bloodshot eyes, and . . . yes . . . and an open sore on its . . . *right* forepaw; that is red, too. And, oh yes; the poor monster, and I do believe it's an old dog . . . it's certainly a misused one . . . almost always has an erection . . . of sorts. That's red, too. And . . . what else? . . . oh, yes; there's a grey-yellow-white colour, too, when he bares his fangs. Like this: Grrrrrrr! Which is what he did when he saw me for the first time . . . the day I moved in. I worried about that animal the very first minute I met him. Now, animals don't take to me like Saint Francis had birds hanging off him all the time. What I mean is: animals are indifferent to me . . . like people (*He smiles slightly*) . . . most of the time. But this dog wasn't indifferent. From the very beginning he'd snarl and then go for me, to get one of my legs. Not like he was rabid, you know; he was sort of a stumbly dog, but he wasn't half-assed, either. It was a good, stumbly run; but I always got away. He got a piece of my trouser leg, look, you can see right here, where it's mended; he got that the second day I lived there; but, I kicked free and got upstairs fast, so that was that. (*Puzzles*) I still don't know to this day how the other roomers manage it, but you know what I *think*: I think it had to do only with me. Cosy. So. Anyway, this went on for over a week, whenever I came in; but never when I went out. That's funny. Or, it *was* funny. I could pack up and live in the street for all the dog cared. Well, I thought about it up in my room one day, one of the times after I'd bolted upstairs, and I made up my mind. I decided: First, I'll kill the dog with kindness, and if that doesn't work . . . I'll just kill him.

(PETER *winces*)

Don't react, Peter; just listen. So, the next day I went out and bought a bag of hamburgers, medium rare, no catsup, no onion; and on the way home I threw away all the rolls and kept just the meat.

(*Action for the following, perhaps*)

When I got back to the rooming-house the dog was waiting for me. I half opened the door that led into the entrance hall, and there he was; waiting for me. It figures. I went in, very cautiously, and I had the hamburgers, you remember; I opened the bag, and I set the meat down about twelve feet from where the dog was snarling at me. Like so! He snarled; stopped snarling; sniffed; moved slowly; then faster; then faster towards the meat. Well, when he got to it he stopped, and he looked at me. I smiled; but tentatively, you understand. He turned his face back to the hamburgers, smelled, sniffed some more, and then . . . RRRAAAA-GGGGGHHHH, like that . . . he tore into them. It was as if he had never eaten anything in his life before, except like garbage. Which might very well have been the truth. I don't think the landlady ever eats anything but garbage. But. He ate all the hamburgers, almost all at once, making sounds in his throat like a woman. *Then* when he'd finished the meat, the hamburger, and tried to eat the paper, too, he sat down and smiled. I think he smiled; I know cats do. It was a very gratifying few moments. Then, BAM, he snarled and made for me again. He didn't get me this time, either. So, I got upstairs, and I lay down on my bed and started to think about the dog again. To be truthful, I was offended, and I was damn mad, too. It was six perfectly good hamburgers with not enough pork in them to make it disgusting. I was offended. But, after a while, I decided to try it for a few more days. If you think about it, this dog had what amounted to an antipathy towards me; really. And, I wondered if I mightn't overcome this antipathy. So, I tried it for five more days, but it was always the same: snarl; sniff; move; faster; stare; gobble; RAAGGGHHH; smile; snarl; BAM. Well, now; by this time Columbus Avenue was strewn with hamburger rolls and I was less offended than disgusted. So, I decided to kill the dog.

(PETER *raises a hand in protest*)

Oh, don't be alarmed, Peter; I didn't succeed. The day I tried to kill the dog I bought only one hamburger and what I thought was a murderous portion of rat poison. When I bought the hamburger I asked the man not to bother with the roll, all I wanted was the meat. I expected some reaction from him, like: we don't sell no hamburgers without rolls; or, wha' d'ya wanna do, eat it out'a ya han's? But no; he smiled benignly, wrapped up the hamburger in waxed paper, and said: A bite for ya pussy-cat? I wanted to say: No, not really; it's part of a plan to poison a dog I know. But, you can't say 'a dog I know' without sounding funny; so I said, a little too loud, I'm afraid, and too formally: YES, A BITE FOR MY PUSSY-CAT. People looked up. It always happens when I try to simplify things; people look up. But that's neither hither nor thither. So. On my way back to the rooming-house, I kneaded the hamburger and rat poison together between my hands, at that point feeling as much sadness as disgust. I opened the door to the entrance hall, and there the monster was, waiting to take the offering and then jump me. Poor bastard; he never learned that the moment he took to smile before he went for me gave me time enough to get out of range. BUT, there he was; malevolence with an erection, waiting. I put the poison patty down, moved towards the stairs and watched. The poor animal gobbled the food down as usual, smiled, which made me almost sick, and then, BAM. But, I sprinted up the stairs, as usual, and the dog didn't get me, as usual. AND IT CAME TO PASS THAT THE BEAST WAS DEATHLY ILL. I knew this because he no longer attended me, and because the landlady sobered up. She stopped me in the hall the same evening of the attempted murder and confided the information that God had struck her puppydog a surely fatal blow. She had forgotten her bewildered lust, and her eyes were wide open for the first time. They looked like the dog's eyes. She snivelled and implored me to pray for the animal. I wanted to say to her: Madam, I have myself to pray for, the coloured queen, the Puerto Rican family, the person in the front room whom I've never seen, the woman who cries deliberately behind her closed door, and the rest of the people in all rooming-houses, everywhere; besides, Madam, I don't understand how to pray. But . . . to simplify things . . . I told her I would pray. She looked up. She said that I was a liar, and that I probably wanted the dog to die. I told her, and there was so much truth here, that I didn't want the dog to die. I didn't, and not just because I'd poisoned him. I'm afraid that I must tell you I wanted the dog to live so that I could see what our new relationship might come to.

(PETER *indicates his increasing displeasure and slowly growing antagonism*)

Please understand, Peter; that sort of thing is important. You must believe me; it *is* important. We have to know the effect of our actions. (*Another deep sigh*) Well, anyway; the dog recovered. I have no idea why, unless he was a descendant of the puppy that guarded the gates of hell or some such resort. I'm not up on my mythology. (*He pronounces the word myth-o-logy*) Are you?

(PETER *sets to thinking, but* JERRY *goes on*)

At any rate, and you've missed the eight-thousand-dollar question, Peter; at any rate, the dog recovered his health and the landlady recovered her thirst, in no way altered by the bow-wow's deliverance. When I came home from a movie that was playing on Forty-second Street, a movie I'd seen, or one that was very much like one or several I'd seen, after the landlady told me puppykins was better, I was so hoping for the dog to be waiting for me. I was . . . well, how would you put it . . . enticed? . . . fascinated? . . . no, I don't think so . . . heart-shatteringly anxious, that's it: I was heart-shatteringly anxious to confront my friend again.

(PETER *reacts scoffingly*)

Yes, Peter; friend. That's the only word for it. I was heart-shatteringly et cetera to confront my doggy friend again. I came in the door and advanced, unafraid, to the centre of the entrance hall. The beast was there . . . looking at me. And, you know, he looked better for his scrape with the nevermind. I stopped; I looked at him; he looked at me. I think . . . I think we stayed a long time that way . . . still, stone-statue . . . just looking at one another. I looked more into his face than he looked into mine. I mean, I can concentrate longer at looking into a dog's face than a dog can concentrate at looking into mine, or into anybody else's face, for that matter. But during that twenty seconds or two hours that we looked into each other's face, we made contact. Now, here is what I had wanted to happen: I loved the dog now, and I wanted him to love me. I had tried to love, and I had tried to kill, and both had been unsuccessful by themselves. I hoped . . . and I don't really know why I expected the dog to understand anything, much less my motivations . . . I hoped that the dog would understand.

(PETER *seems to be hypnotized*)

It's just . . . it's just that . . . (JERRY *is abnormally tense, now*) . . . it's just that if you can't deal with people, you have to make a start somewhere. WITH ANIMALS! (*Much faster now, and like a conspirator*) Don't you see? A person has to have some way of dealing with SOMETHING. If not with people . . . SOMETHING. With a bed, with a cockroach, with a mirror . . . no, that's too hard, that's one of the last steps. With a cockroach, with a . . . with a . . . with a carpet, a roll of toilet paper . . . no, not that, either . . . that's a mirror, too; always check bleeding. You see how hard it is to find things? With a street corner, and too many lights, all colours reflecting on the oily-wet streets . . . with a wisp of smoke, a wisp . . . of smoke . . . with . . . with pornographic playing-cards, with a strong-box . . . WITHOUT A LOCK . . . with love, with vomiting, with crying, with fury because the pretty little ladies aren't pretty little ladies, with making money with your body which is an act of love and I could prove it, with howling because you're alive; with God. How about that? WITH GOD WHO IS A COLOURED QUEEN WHO WEARS A KIMONO AND PLUCKS HIS EYEBROWS! WHO IS A WOMAN WHO CRIES WITH DETERMINATION BEHIND HER CLOSED DOOR . . . with God who, I'm told, turned his back on the whole thing some time ago . . . with . . . some day, with people. (JERRY *sighs the next word heavily*) People. With an idea; a concept. And where better, where ever better in this humiliating excuse for a jail, where better to communicate one single, simple-minded idea than in an entrance hall? Where? It would be A START! Where better to make a beginning . . . to understand and just possibly be understood . . . a beginning of an understanding, than with . . . (*Here* JERRY *seems to fall into almost grotesque fatigue*) . . . than with A DOG. Just that; a dog. (*Here there is a silence that might be prolonged for a moment or so; then* JERRY *wearily finishes his story*) A dog. It seemed like a perfectly sensible idea. Man is a dog's best friend, remember. So: the dog and I looked at each other. I longer than the dog. And what I saw then has been the same ever since. Whenever the dog and I see each other we both stop where we are. We regard each other with a mixture of sadness and suspicion, and then we feign indifference. We walk past each other safely; we have an understanding. It's very sad, but you'll have to admit that it is an understanding. We had made many attempts at contact, and we had failed. The dog has returned to garbage, and I to solitary but free passage. I have not returned. I mean to say, I have *gained* solitary free passage, if that much further loss can be said to be gain. I have learned that neither kindness nor cruelty by themselves, independent of each other, creates any effect beyond themselves; and I have learned that the two combined, together, at the same time, are the teaching emotion. And what is gained is loss. And what has been the result: the dog and I have attained a compromise; more of a bargain, really. We neither love nor hurt because we do not try to reach each other. And, *was* trying to feed the dog an act of love? And, perhaps, was the dog's attempt to bite me *not* an act of love? If we can so misunderstand, well then, why have we invented the word love in the first place?

(*There is silence.* JERRY *moves to Peter's bench and sits down beside him. This is the first time Jerry has sat down during the play*)

The Story of Jerry and the Dog: the end.

(PETER *is silent*)

Well, Peter? (JERRY *is suddenly cheerful*) Well, Peter? Do you think I could sell that story to the *Reader's Digest* and make a couple of hundred bucks for *The Most Unforgettable Character I've Ever Met*? Huh?

(JERRY *is animated, but* PETER *is disturbed*)

Oh, come on now, Peter; tell me what you think.

PETER (*numb*): I . . . I don't understand what . . . I don't think I . . . (*Now almost tearfully*) Why did you tell me all of this?

JERRY: Why not?

PETER: I DON'T UNDERSTAND!

JERRY (*furious, but whispering*): That's a lie.

PETER: No. No, it's not.

JERRY (*quietly*): I tried to explain it to you as I went along. I went slowly; it all has to do with . . .

PETER: I DON'T WANT TO HEAR ANY MORE. I don't understand you, or your landlady, or her dog . . .

JERRY: *Her* dog! I thought it was my . . . No. No, you're right. It *is* her dog. (*Looks at* PETER *intently, shaking his head*) I don't know what I was thinking about; of course you don't understand. (*In a monotone, wearily*) I don't live in your block; I'm not married to two parakeets, or whatever your set-up is. I am a *permanent transient*, and my home is the sickening rooming-houses on the West Side of New York City, which is the greatest city in the world. Amen.

PETER: I'm . . . I'm sorry; I didn't mean to . . .

JERRY: Forget it. I suppose you don't quite know what to make of me, eh?

PETER (*a joke*): We get all kinds in publishing. (*Chuckles*)

JERRY: You're a funny man. (*He forces a laugh*) You know that? You're a very . . . a richly comic person.

PETER (*modestly, but amused*): Oh, now, not really. (*Still chuckling*)

JERRY: Peter, do I annoy you, or confuse you?

PETER (*lightly*): Well, I must confess that this wasn't the kind of afternoon I'd anticipated.

JERRY: You mean, I'm not the gentleman you were expecting.

PETER: I wasn't expecting anybody.

JERRY: No, I don't imagine you were. But I'm here, and I'm

not leaving.

PETER (*consulting his watch*): Well, you may not be, but I must be getting home soon.

JERRY: Oh, come on; stay a while longer.

PETER: I really should get home; you see . . .

JERRY (*tickles Peter's ribs with his fingers*): Oh, come on.

(PETER *is very ticklish; as* JERRY *continues to tickle him his voice becomes falsetto*)

PETER: No, I . . . OHHHHH! Don't do that. Stop, Stop. Ohhh, no, no.

JERRY: Oh, come on.

PETER (*as* JERRY *tickles*): Oh, hee, hee, hee. I must go. I . . . hee, hee, hee. After all, stop, stop, hee, hee, hee, after all, the parakeets will be getting dinner ready soon. Hee, hee. And the cats are setting the table. Stop, stop, and, and . . . (*He is beside himself now*) . . . and we're having . . . hee, hee . . . uh . . . ho, ho, ho.

(JERRY *stops tickling Peter, but the combination of the tickling and his own mad whimsy has* PETER *laughing almost hysterically. As his laughter continues, then subsides,* JERRY *watches him, with a curious fixed smile*)

JERRY: Peter?

PETER: Oh, ha, ha, ha, ha, ha. What? What?

JERRY: Listen, now.

PETER: Oh, ho, ho. What . . . what is it, Jerry? Oh, my.

JERRY (*mysteriously*): Peter, do you want to know what happened at the zoo?

PETER: Ah, ha, ha. The what? Oh, yes; the zoo. Oh, ho, ho. Well, I had my own zoo there for a moment with . . . hee, hee, the parakeets getting dinner ready, and the . . . ha, ha, whatever it was, the . . .

JERRY (*calmly*): Yes, that was very funny, Peter. I wouldn't have expected it. But do you want to hear what happened at the zoo, or not?

PETER: Yes. Yes, by all means; tell me what happened at the zoo. Oh, my. I don't know what happened to me.

JERRY: Now I'll let you in on what happened at the zoo; but first, I should tell you why I went to the zoo. I went to the zoo to find out more about the way people exist with animals, and the way animals exist with each other, and with people too. It probably wasn't a fair test, what with everyone separated by bars from everyone else, the animals for the most part from each other, and always the people from the animals. But, if it's a zoo, that's the way it is. (*He pokes Peter on the arm*) Move over.

PETER (*friendly*): I'm sorry, haven't you enough room? (*He shifts a little*)

JERRY (*smiling slightly*): Well, all the animals are there, and all the people are there, and it's Sunday and all the children are there. (*He pokes Peter again*) Move over.

PETER (*patiently, still friendly*): All right.

(*He moves some more, and* JERRY *has all the room he might need*)

JERRY: And it's a hot day, so all the stench is there, too, and all the balloon sellers, and all the ice-cream sellers, and all the seals are barking, and all the birds are screaming. (*Pokes Peter harder*) Move over!

PETER (*beginning to be annoyed*): Look here, you have more than enough room! (*But he moves more, and is now fairly cramped at one end of the bench*)

JERRY: And I am there, and it's feeding time at the lion's house, and the lion keeper comes into the lion cage, one of the lion cages, to feed one of the lions. (*Punches Peter on the arm, hard*) MOVE OVER!

PETER (*very annoyed*): I can't move over any more, and stop hitting me. What's the matter with you?

JERRY: Do you want to hear the story? (*Punches Peter's arm again*)

PETER (*flabbergasted*): I'm not so sure! I certainly don't want to be punched in the arm.

JERRY (*punches Peter's arm again*): Like that?

PETER: Stop it. What's the matter with you?

JERRY: I'm crazy, you bastard.

PETER: That isn't funny.

JERRY: Listen to me, Peter. I want this bench. You go sit on the bench over there, and if you're good I'll tell you the rest of the story.

PETER (*flustered*): But . . . what ever for? What *is* the matter with you? Besides, I see no reason why I should give up this bench. I sit on this bench almost every Sunday afternoon, in good weather. It's secluded here; there's never anyone sitting here, so I have it all to myself.

JERRY (*softly*): Get off this bench, Peter; I want it.

PETER (*almost whining*): No.

JERRY: I said I want this bench, and I'm going to have it. Now get over there.

PETER: People can't have everything they want. You should know that; it's a rule; people can have some of the things they want, but they can't have everything.

JERRY (*laughs*): Imbecile! You're slow-witted!

PETER: Stop that!

JERRY: You're a vegetable! Go lie down on the ground.

PETER (*intense*): Now *you* listen to me. I've put up with you all afternoon.

JERRY: Not really.

PETER: LONG ENOUGH. I've put up with you long enough. I've listened to you because you seemed . . . well, because I thought you wanted to talk to somebody.

JERRY: You put things well; economically, and, yet . . . oh, what is the word I want to put justice to your . . . JESUS, you make me sick . . . get off here and give me my bench.

PETER: MY BENCH!

JERRY (*pushes Peter almost, but not quite, off the bench*): Get out of my sight.

PETER (*regaining his position*): God da . . . mn you. That's enough! I've had enough of you. I will not give up this bench; you can't have it, and that's that. Now, go away.

(JERRY *snorts but does not move*)

Go away, I said.

(JERRY *does not move*)

Get away from here. If you don't move on . . . you're a bum . . . that's what you are . . . If you don't move on, I'll get a policeman here and make you go.

(JERRY *laughs, stays*)

I warn you, I'll call a policeman.

JERRY (*softly*): You won't find a policeman around here; they're all over on the west side of the park chasing fairies down from the trees or out of the bushes. That's all they do. That's their function. So scream your head off; it won't do you any good.

PETER: POLICE! I warn you, I'll have you arrested. POLICE! (*Pause*) I said POLICE! (*Pause*) I feel ridiculous.

JERRY: You look ridiculous: a grown man screaming for the police on a bright Sunday afternoon in the park with nobody harming you. If a policeman *did* fill his quota and come sludging over this way he'd probably take you in as a nut.

PETER (*with disgust and impotence*): Great God, I just came here to read, and now you want me to give up the bench. You're mad.

JERRY: Hey, I got news for you, as they say. I'm on your precious bench, and you're never going to have it for yourself again.

PETER (*furious*): Look, you; get off my bench. I don't care if it makes any sense or not. I want this bench to myself; I want you OFF IT!

JERRY (*mocking*): Aw . . . look who's mad.

PETER: GET OUT!

JERRY: No.

PETER: I WARN YOU!

JERRY: Do you know how ridiculous you look *now*?

PETER (*his fury and self-consciousness have possessed him*): It doesn't matter. (*He is almost crying*) GET AWAY FROM MY BENCH!

JERRY: Why? You have everything in the world you want; you've told me about your home, and your family, and *your own* little zoo. You have everything, and now you want this bench. Are these the things men fight for? Tell me, Peter, is this bench, this iron and this wood, is this your honour? Is this the thing in the world you'd fight for? Can you think of anything more absurd?

PETER: Absurd? Look, I'm not going to talk to you about honour, or even try to explain it to you. Besides, it isn't a question of honour; but even if it were, you wouldn't understand.

JERRY (*contemptuously*): You don't even know what you're saying, do you? This is probably the first time in your life you've had anything more trying to face than changing your cats' toilet box. Stupid! Don't you have any idea, not even the slightest, what other people *need*?

PETER: Oh, boy, listen to you; well, you don't need this bench. That's for sure.

JERRY: Yes; yes, I do.

PETER (*quivering*): I've come here for years; I have hours of great pleasure, great satisfaction, right here. And that's important to a man. I'm a responsible person, and I'm a GROWN-UP. This is my bench, and you have no right to take it away from me.

JERRY: Fight for it, then. Defend yourself; defend your bench.

PETER: You've *pushed* me to it. Get up and fight.

JERRY: Like a man?

PETER (*still angry*): Yes, like a man, if you insist on mocking me even further.

JERRY: I'll have to give you credit for one thing: you *are* a vegetable, and a slightly near-sighted one, I think . . .

PETER: THAT'S ENOUGH . . .

JERRY: . . . but, you know, as they say on TV all the time— you know—and I mean this, Peter, you have a certain dignity; it surprises me . . .

PETER: STOP!

JERRY (*rises lazily*): Very well, Peter, we'll battle for the bench, but we're not evenly matched. (*He takes out and clicks open an ugly-looking knife*)

PETER (*suddenly awakening to the reality of the situation*): You *are* mad! You're stark raving mad! YOU'RE GOING TO KILL ME!

(*But before Peter has time to think what to do,* JERRY *tosses the knife at Peter's feet*)

JERRY: There you go. Pick it up. You have the knife and we'll be more evenly matched.

PETER (*horrified*): No!

(JERRY *rushes over to Peter, grabs him by the collar;* PETER *rises; their faces almost touch*)

JERRY: Now you pick up that knife and you fight with me. You fight for your self-respect; you fight for that god-damned bench.

PETER (*struggling*): No! Let . . . let go of me! He . . . Help!

JERRY (*slaps Peter on each 'fight'*): You fight, you miserable bastard; fight for that bench; fight for your parakeets; fight for your cats; fight for your two daughters; fight for your wife; fight for your manhood, you pathetic little vegetable. (*Spits in Peter's face*) You couldn't even get your wife with a male child.

PETER (*breaks away, enraged*): It's a matter of genetics, not manhood, you . . . you monster. (*He darts down, picks up the knife and backs off a little; breathing heavily*) I'll give you one last chance; get out of here and leave me alone! (*He holds the knife with a firm arm, but far in front of him, not to attack, but to defend*)

JERRY (*sighs heavily*): So be it!

(*With a rush he charges Peter and impales himself on the knife. Tableau: For just a moment, complete silence, Jerry impaled on the knife at the end of Peter's still firm arm. Then* PETER *screams, pulls away, leaving the knife in Jerry.* JERRY *is motionless, on point. Then he, too, screams, and it must be the sound of an infuriated and fatally wounded animal. With the knife in him, he stumbles back to the bench that Peter had vacated. He crumbles there, sitting, facing Peter, his eyes wide in agony, his mouth open*)

PETER (*whispering*): Oh my God, oh my God, oh my God . . .

(PETER *repeats these words many times, very rapidly.* JERRY *is dying; but now his expression seems to change. His features relax, and while his voice varies, sometimes wrenched with pain, for the most part he seems removed from his dying. He smiles*)

JERRY: Thank you, Peter. I mean that, now; thank you very much.

(PETER'S *mouth drops open. He cannot move; he is transfixed*)

Oh, Peter, I was so afraid I'd drive you away. (*He laughs as best he can*) You don't know how afraid I was you'd go away and leave me. And now I'll tell you what happened at the zoo. I think . . . I think this is what happened at the zoo . . . I think. I think that while I was at the zoo I decided that I would walk north . . . northerly, rather . . . until I found you . . . or somebody . . . and I decided that

I would talk to you . . . I would tell you things . . . and things that I would tell you would . . . Well, here we are. You see? Here we *are*. But . . . I don't know . . . could I have planned all this? No . . . no, I couldn't have. But I think I did. And now I've told you what you wanted to know, haven't I? And now you know all about what happened at the zoo. And now you know what you'll see in your TV, and the face I told you about . . . you re-member . . . the face I told you about . . . my face, the face you see right now. Peter . . . Peter? . . . Peter . . . thank you. I came unto you (*He laughs, so faintly*) and you have comforted me. Dear Peter.

PETER (*almost fainting*): Oh my God!

JERRY: You'd better go now. Somebody might come by, and you don't want to be here when anyone comes.

PETER (*does not move, but begins to weep*): Oh my God, oh my God.

JERRY (*most faintly, now; he is very near death*): You won't be coming back here any more, Peter; you've been dispossessed. You've lost your bench, but you've defended your honour. And Peter, I'll tell you something now; you're not really a vegetable; it's all right, you're an animal. You're an animal, too. But you'd better hurry now, Peter. Hurry, you'd better go . . . see? (JERRY *takes a handkerchief and with great effort and pain wipes the knife handle clean of fingerprints*) Hurry away, Peter.

(PETER *begins to stagger away*)

Wait . . . wait, Peter. Take your book . . . book. Right here . . . beside me . . . on your bench . . . my bench, rather. Come . . . take your book.

(PETER *starts for the book, but retreats*)

Hurry . . . Peter.

(PETER *rushes to the bench, grabs the book, retreats*)

Very good, Peter . . . very good. Now . . . hurry away.

(PETER *hesitates for a moment, then flees, stage-left*)

Hurry away . . . (*His eyes are closed now*) Hurry away, your parakeets are making the dinner . . . the cats . . . are setting the table . . .

PETER (*off-stage, a pitiful howl*): OH, MY GOD!

JERRY (*his eyes still closed, he shakes his head and speaks; a combination of scornful mimicry and supplication*): Oh . . . my . . .God. (*He is dead*)

CURTAIN

REVUE SKETCHES

Harold Pinter

TROUBLE IN THE WORKS

An office in a factory. MR FIBBS *at the desk. A knock at the*
door. Enter MR WILLS.

FIBBS: Ah, Wills. Good. Come in. Sit down, will you?
WILLS: Thanks, Mr Fibbs.
FIBBS: You got my message?
WILLS: I just got it.
FIBBS: Good. Good.

Pause.

Good. Well now . . . Have a cigar?
WILLS: No, thanks, not for me, Mr Fibbs.
FIBBS: Well, now, Wills, I hear there's been a little trouble in
the factory.
WILLS: Yes, I . . . I suppose you could call it that, Mr Fibbs.
FIBBS: Well, what in heaven's name is it all about?
WILLS: Well, I don't exactly know how to put it, Mr Fibbs.
FIBBS: Now come on, Wills, I've got to know what it is, before
I can do anything about it.
WILLS: Well, Mr Fibbs, it's simply a matter that the men have
. . . well, they seem to have taken a turn against some of
the products.
FIBBS: Taken a turn?
WILLS: They just don't seem to like them much any more.
FIBBS: Don't like them? But we've got the reputation of having the finest machine part turnover in the country. They're
the best paid men in the industry. We've got the cheapest
canteen in Yorkshire. No two menus are alike. We've got a
billiard hall, haven't we, on the premises, we've got a
swimming pool for use of staff. And what about the long-
playing record room? And you tell me they're dissatisfied?
WILLS: Oh, the men are very grateful for all the amenities,
sir. They just don't like the products.

FIBBS: But they're beautiful products. I've been in the business a lifetime. I've never seen such beautiful products.

WILLS: There it is, sir.

FIBBS: Which ones don't they like?

WILLS: Well, there's the brass pet cock, for instance.

FIBBS: The brass pet cock? What's the matter with the brass pet cock?

WILLS: They just don't seem to like it any more.

FIBBS: But what exactly don't they like about it?

WILLS: Perhaps it's just the look of it.

FIBBS: That brass pet cock? But I tell you it's perfection. Nothing short of perfection.

WILLS: They've just gone right off it.

FIBBS: Well, I'm flabbergasted.

WILLS: It's not only the brass pet cock, Mr Fibbs.

FIBBS: What else?

WILLS: There's the hemi unibal spherical rod end.

FIBBS: The hemi unibal spherical rod end? Where could you find a finer rod end?

WILLS: There are rod ends and rod ends, Mr Fibbs.

FIBBS: I know there are rod ends and rod ends. But where could you find a finer hemi unibal spherical rod end?

WILLS: They just don't want to have anything more to do with it.

FIBBS: This is shattering. Shattering. What else? Come on, Wills. There's no point in hiding anything from me.

WILLS: Well, I hate to say it, but they've gone very vicious about the high speed taper shank spiral flute reamers.

FIBBS: The high speed taper shank spiral flute reamers! But that's absolutely ridiculous! What could they possibly have against the high speed taper shank spiral flute reamers?

WILLS: All I can say is they're in a state of very bad agitation about them. And then there's the gunmetal side outlet relief with handwheel.

FIBBS: What!

WILLS: There's the nippled connector and the nippled adaptor and the vertical mechanical comparator.

FIBBS: No!

WILLS: And the one they can't speak about without trembling is the jaw for Jacob's chuck for use on portable drill.

FIBBS: My own Jacob's chuck? Not my very own Jacob's chuck?

WILLS: They've just taken a turn against the whole lot of them, I tell you. Male elbow adaptors, tubing nuts, grub screws, internal fan washers, dog points, half dog points, white metal bushes—

FIBBS: But not, surely not, my lovely parallel male stud couplings.

WILLS: They hate and detest your lovely parallel male stud couplings, and the straight flange pump connectors, and back nuts, and front nuts, *and* the bronzedraw off cock with handwheel and the bronzedraw off cock without handwheel!

FIBBS: Not the bronzedraw off cock with handwheel?

WILLS: And without handwheel.

FIBBS: Without handwheel?

WILLS: And with handwheel.

FIBBS: Not with handwheel?

WILLS: And without handwheel.

FIBBS: Without handwheel?

WILLS: With handwheel *and* without handwheel.

FIBBS: With handwheel *and* without handwheel?

WILLS: With or without!

Pause.

FIBBS (*broken*): Tell me. What do they want to make in its place?

WILLS: Brandy balls.

THE BLACK AND WHITE

The FIRST OLD WOMAN *is sitting at a milk bar table. Small.*
A SECOND OLD WOMAN *approaches. Tall. She is carrying two*
bowls of soup, which are covered by two plates, on each of
which is a slice of bread. She puts the bowls down on the
table carefully.

SECOND: You see that one come up and speak to me at the
counter?

She takes the bread plates off the bowls, takes two
spoons from her pocket, and places the bowls, plates and
spoons.

FIRST: You got the bread, then?
SECOND: I didn't know how I was going to carry it. In the end
I put the plates on top of the soup.
FIRST: I like a bit of bread with my soup.

They begin the soup. Pause.

SECOND: Did you see that one come up and speak to me at
the counter?
FIRST: Who?
SECOND: Comes up to me, he says, hullo, he says, what's the
time by your clock? Bloody liberty. I was just standing there
getting your soup.
FIRST: It's tomato soup.
SECOND: What's the time by your clock? he says.
FIRST: I bet you answered him back.
SECOND: I told him all right. Go on, I said, why don't you
get back into your scraghole, I said, clear off out of it before
I call a copper.

Pause.

FIRST: I not long got here.

SECOND: Did you get the all-night bus?

FIRST: I got the all-night bus straight here.

SECOND: Where from?

FIRST: Marble Arch.

SECOND: Which one?

FIRST: The two-nine-four, that takes me all the way to Fleet Street.

SECOND: So does the two-nine-one. (*Pause*) I see you talking to two strangers as I come in. You want to stop talking to strangers, old piece of boot like you, you mind who you talk to.

FIRST: I wasn't talking to any strangers.

Pause. The FIRST OLD WOMAN *follows the progress of a bus through the window.*

That's another all-night bus gone down. (*Pause*) Going up the other way. Fulham way. (*Pause*) That was a two-nine-seven. (*Pause*) I've never been up that way. (*Pause*) I've been down to Liverpool Street.

SECOND: That's up the other way.

FIRST: I don't fancy going down there, down Fulham way, and all up there.

SECOND: Uh-uh.

FIRST: I've never fancied that direction much.

Pause.

SECOND: How's your bread?

Pause.

FIRST: Eh?

SECOND: Your bread.

FIRST: All right. How's yours?

Pause.

SECOND: They don't charge for the bread if you have soup.
FIRST: They do if you have tea.
SECOND: If you have tea they do. (*Pause*) You talk to strangers
    they'll take you in. Mind my word. Coppers'll take you in.
FIRST: I don't talk to strangers.
SECOND: They took me away in the wagon once.
FIRST: They didn't keep you though.
SECOND: They didn't keep me, but that was only because
    they took a fancy to me. They took a fancy to me when
    they got me in the wagon.
FIRST: Do you think they'd take a fancy to me?
SECOND: I wouldn't back on it.

The FIRST OLD WOMAN *gazes out of the window.*

FIRST: You can see what goes on from this top table.
    (*Pause*) It's better than going down to that place on the
    embankment, anyway.
SECOND: Yes, there's not too much noise.
FIRST: There's always a bit of noise.
SECOND: Yes, there's always a bit of life.

Pause.

FIRST: They'll be closing down soon to give it a scrub-round.
SECOND: There's a wind out.

Pause.

FIRST: I wouldn't mind staying.
SECOND: They won't let you.
FIRST: I know. (*Pause*) Still, they only close hour and half,
    don't they? (*Pause*) It's not long. (*Pause*) You can go along,
    then come back.
SECOND: I'm going. I'm not coming back.

FIRST: When it's light I come back. Have my tea.

SECOND: I'm going. I'm going up to the Garden.

FIRST: I'm not going down there. (*Pause*) I'm going up to Waterloo Bridge.

SECOND: You'll just about see the last two-nine-six come up over the river.

FIRST: I'll just catch a look of it. Time I get up there.

Pause.

It don't look like an all-night bus in daylight, do it?

REQUEST STOP

A queue at a Request Bus Stop. A WOMAN *at the head, with a* SMALL MAN *in a raincoat next to her, two other* WOMEN *and a* MAN.

WOMAN (*to* SMALL MAN): I beg your pardon, what did you say?

Pause.

All I asked you was if I could get a bus from here to Shepherds Bush.

Pause.

Nobody asked you to start making insinuations.

Pause.

Who do you think you are?

Pause.

Huh. I know your sort, I know your type. Don't worry, I know all about people like you.

Pause.

We can all tell where you come from. They're putting your sort inside every day of the week.

Pause.

All I've got to do, is report you, and you'd be standing in the dock in next to no time. One of my best friends is a plain clothes detective.

Pause.

I know all about it. Standing there as if butter wouldn't melt in your mouth. Meet you in a dark alley it'd be . . . another story. (*To the others, who stare into space*) You heard what this man said to me. All I asked him was if I could get a bus from here to Shepherds Bush. (*To him*) I've got witnesses, don't you worry about that.

Pause.

Impertinence.

Pause.

Ask a man a civil question he treats you like a threepenny bit. (*To him*) I've got better things to do my lad, I can assure you. I'm not going to stand here and be insulted on a public highway. Anyone can tell you're a foreigner. I was born just around the corner. Anyone can tell you're just up from the country for a bit of a lark. I know your sort.

Pause.

She goes to a LADY.

Excuse me lady. I'm thinking of taking this man up to the magistrate's court, you heard him make that crack, would you like to be a witness?

The LADY *steps into the road.*

LADY: Taxi . . .

She disappears.

WOMAN: We know what sort she is. (*Back to position*) I was the first in this queue.

Pause.

Born just round the corner. Born and bred. These people from the country haven't the faintest idea of how to behave. Peruvians. You're bloody lucky I don't put you on a charge. You ask a straightforward question— •

The others suddenly thrust out their arms at a passing bus. They run off left after it. The WOMAN, *alone, clicks her teeth and mutters. A man walks from the right to the stop, and waits. She looks at him out of the corner of her eye. At length she speaks shyly, hesitantly, with a slight smile.*

Excuse me. Do you know if I can get a bus from here . . . to Marble Arch?

LAST TO GO

A coffee stall. A BARMAN *and an old* NEWSPAPER SELLER. *The* BARMAN *leans on his counter, the* OLD MAN *stands with tea. Silence.*

MAN: You was a bit busier earlier.
BARMAN: Ah.
MAN: Round about ten.
BARMAN: Ten, was it?
MAN: About then.

Pause.

I passed by here about then.
BARMAN: Oh yes?
MAN: I noticed you were doing a bit of trade.

Pause.

BARMAN: Yes, trade was very brisk here about ten.
MAN: Yes, I noticed.

Pause.

I sold my last one about then. Yes. About nine forty-five.
BARMAN: Sold your last then, did you?
MAN: Yes, my last 'Evening News' it was. Went about twenty to ten.

Pause.

BARMAN: 'Evening News', was it?
MAN: Yes.

Pause.

Sometimes it's the 'Star' is the last to go.
BARMAN: Ah.
MAN: Or the . . . whatisname.
BARMAN: 'Standard'.
MAN: Yes.

   Pause.

All I had left tonight was the 'Evening News'.

   Pause.

BARMAN: Then that went, did it?
MAN: Yes.

   Pause.

Like a shot.

   Pause.

BARMAN: You didn't have any left, eh?
MAN: No. Not after I sold that one.

   Pause.

BARMAN: It was after that you must have come by here then, was it?
MAN: Yes, I come by here after that, see, after I packed up.
BARMAN: You didn't stop here though, did you?
MAN: When?
BARMAN: I mean, you didn't stop here and have a cup of tea then, did you?
MAN: What, about ten?
BARMAN: Yes.
MAN: No, I went up to Victoria.
BARMAN: No, I thought I didn't see you.

MAN: I had to go up to Victoria.

Pause.

BARMAN: Yes, trade was very brisk here about then.

Pause.

MAN: I went to see if I could get hold of George.
BARMAN: Who?
MAN: George.

Pause.

BARMAN: George who?
MAN: George . . . whatisname.
BARMAN: Oh.

Pause.

   Did you get hold of him?
MAN: No. No, I couldn't get hold of him. I couldn't locate him.
BARMAN: He's not about much now, is he?

Pause.

MAN: When did you last see him then?
BARMAN: Oh, I haven't seen him for years.
MAN: No, nor me.

Pause.

BARMAN: Used to suffer very bad from arthritis.
MAN: Arthritis?
BARMAN: Yes.
MAN: He never suffered from arthritis.

BARMAN: Suffered very bad.

Pause.

MAN: Not when I knew him.

Pause.

BARMAN: I think he must have left the area.

Pause.

MAN: Yes, it was the 'Evening News' was the last to go tonight.
BARMAN: Not always the last though, is it, though?
MAN: No. Oh no. I mean sometimes it's the 'News'. Other times it's one of the others. No way of telling beforehand. Until you've got your last one left, of course. Then you can tell which one it's going to be.
BARMAN: Yes.

Pause.

MAN: Oh yes.

Pause.

I think he must have left the area.

APPLICANT

An office. LAMB, *a young man, eager, cheerful, enthusiastic, is striding nervously, alone. The door opens.* MISS PIFFS *comes in. She is the essence of efficiency.*

PIFFS: Ah, good morning.
LAMB: Oh, good morning, miss.
PIFFS: Are you Mr Lamb?
LAMB: That's right.
PIFFS (*studying a sheet of paper*): Yes. You're applying for this vacant post, aren't you?
LAMB: I am actually, yes.
PIFFS: Are you a physicist?
LAMB: Oh yes, indeed. It's my whole life.
PIFFS (*languidly*): Good. Now our procedure is, that before we discuss the applicant's qualifications we like to subject him to a little test to determine his psychological suitability. You've no objection?
LAMB: Oh, good heavens, no.
PIFFS: Jolly good.

MISS PIFFS *has taken some objects out of a drawer and goes to* LAMB. *She places a chair for him.*

PIFFS: Please sit down. (*He sits*) Can I fit these to your palms?
LAMB (*affably*): What are they?
PIFFS: Electrodes.
LAMB: Oh yes, of course. Funny little things.

She attaches them to his palms.

PIFFS: Now the earphones.

She attaches earphones to his head.

LAMB: I say how amusing.
PIFFS: Now I plug in.

She plugs in to the wall.

LAMB (*a trifle nervously*): Plug in, do you? Oh yes, of course. Yes, you'd have to, wouldn't you?

MISS PIFFS *perches on a high stool and looks down on* LAMB.

This helps to determine my . . . my suitability does it?
PIFFS: Unquestionably. Now relax. Just relax. Don't think about a thing.
LAMB: No.
PIFFS: Relax completely. Rela-a-a-x. Quite relaxed?

LAMB *nods.* MISS PIFFS *presses a button on the side of her stool. A piercing high pitched buzz-hum is heard.* LAMB *jolts rigid. His hands go to his earphones. He is propelled from the chair. He tries to crawl under the chair.* MISS PIFFS *watches, impassive. The noise stops.* LAMB *peeps out from under the chair, crawls out, stands, twitches, emits a short chuckle and collapses in the chair.*

PIFFS: Would you say you were an excitable person?
LAMB: Not—not unduly, no. Of course, I—
PIFFS: Would you say you were a moody person?
LAMB: Moody? No, I wouldn't say I was moody—well, sometimes occasionally I—
PIFFS: Do you ever get fits of depression?
LAMB: Well, I wouldn't call them depression exactly—
PIFFS: Do you often do things you regret in the morning?
LAMB: Regret? Things I regret? Well, it depends what you mean by often, really—I mean when you say often—
PIFFS: Are you often puzzled by women?
LAMB: Women?

PIFFS: Men.

LAMB: Men? Well, I was just going to answer the question about women—

PIFFS: Do you often feel puzzled?

LAMB: Puzzled?

PIFFS: By women.

LAMB: Women?

PIFFS: Men.

LAMB: Oh, now just a minute, I . . . Look, do you want separate answers or a joint answer?

PIFFS: After your day's work do you ever feel tired? Edgy? Fretty? Irritable? At a loose end? Morose? Frustrated? Morbid? Unable to concentrate? Unable to sleep? Unable to eat? Unable to remain seated? Unable to remain upright? Lustful? Indolent? On heat? Randy? Full of desire? Full of energy? Full of dread? Drained? of energy, of dread? or desire?

   Pause.

LAMB (*thinking*): Well, it's difficult to say really . . .

PIFFS: Are you a good mixer?

LAMB: Well, you've touched on quite an interesting point there—

PIFFS: Do you suffer from eczema, listlessness, or falling coat?

LAMB: Er . . .

PIFFS: Are you virgo intacta?

LAMB: I beg your pardon?

PIFFS: Are you virgo intacta?

LAMB: Oh, I say, that's rather embarrassing. I mean—in front of a lady—

PIFFS: Are you virgo intacta?

LAMB: Yes, I am, actually. I'll make no secret of it.

PIFFS: Have you always been virgo intacta?

LAMB: Oh yes, always. Always.

PIFFS: From the word go?

LAMB: Go? Oh yes, from the word go.
PIFFS: Do women frighten you?

She presses a button on the other side of her stool. The stage is plunged into redness, which flashes on and off in time with her questions.

PIFFS (*building*): Their clothes? Their shoes? Their voices? Their laughter? Their stares? Their way of walking? Their way of sitting? Their way of smiling? Their way of talking? Their mouths? Their hands? Their feet? Their shins? Their thighs? Their knees? Their eyes?
Their (*Drumbeat*): Their (*Drumbeat*). Their (*Cymbal bang*). Their (*Trombone chord*). Their (*Bass note*).
LAMB (*in a high voice*): Well it depends what you mean really—

The light still flashes. She presses the other button and the piercing buzz-hum is heard again. LAMB'S *hands go to his earphones. He is propelled from the chair, falls, rolls, crawls, totters and collapses.*

Silence.

He lies face upwards. MISS PIFFS *looks at him then walks to* LAMB *and bends over him.*

PIFFS: Thank you very much, Mr Lamb. We'll let you know.

IF YOU'RE GLAD I'LL BE FRANK

Tom Stoppard

CHARACTERS

LAURA LOGAN
MCNEE
MISS PARKER
MAX

Place
Laura Logan's flat in Marble Arch Mansions, W2.
Time
Friday morning.

IF YOU'RE GLAD I'LL BE FRANK

From her first words it is apparent that GLADYS *is the* TIM *girl, and always has been.*

As such, she has two columns to herself.

The right-hand column is for the Speaking Clock, and as such it is ostensibly continuous. But of course we hear her voice direct, not through a telephone unless otherwise indicated.

The left-hand column is for her unspoken thoughts, and of course this one has the dominant value.

It should be obvious in the script when her TIM *voice is needed in the background as counterpoint, and when it should be drowned altogether by the rising dominance of her thoughts.*

When her TIM *voice intrudes again I have indicated this not by the actual words she uses, because the actual time she announces should be related to the number of minutes or seconds that have passed (ie depending on the pace of the broadcast) but by suggesting the* space of time *that her speaking voice should take up, and this appears in the script in this form: (3-4 seconds).*

GLADYS *operates the pips too, and these are indicated thus: (*PIP PIP PIP*).*

Some of GLADYS*'s sustained passages fall into something half-way between prose and verse, and I have gone some way to indicate the rhythms by line-endings, but of course the effect should not be declamatory.*

SCENE 1

FRANK, *who turns out to be a bus driver, is heard dialling* "TIM".

> GLADYS (*through phone*):
> At the third stroke it will

be eight fifty-nine pre-
cisely.

FRANK (*amazed disbelief*): It
can't be . . .

(PIP PIP PIP)

. . . At the third stroke it
will be eight fifty-nine
and ten seconds . . .

(*Fearful hope*): It's
not . . .?

(PIP PIP PIP)

. . . At the third stroke it
will be eight fifty-nine
and twenty seconds . . .

(*Joy*) It is! . . . *Gladys!*
It's my Gladys! (*Fade*)

(PIP PIP PIP)

SCENE 2

Exterior mid traffic, Big Ben begins its nine a.m. routine.
Cut to interior: no traffic, Big Ben fainter.

PORTER (*murmurs*): Nine o'clock. Here we go. (*What happens*
is this: MYRTLE, MORTIMER, COURTENAY-SMITH,   SIR
JOHN *and the* FIRST LORD OF THE POST OFFICE (LORD
COOT) *enter from the street on the first, third, fifth,*
seventh and ninth strokes of Big Ben respectively (the
second, fourth, sixth and eighth strokes being heard
through the closed door). Each opening of the door lets
in traffic sound momentarily and amplifies Big Ben)
(*Street door*)
PORTER: Morning, Mrs Trelawney.
MYRTLE (*gay*): Hello, Tommy.

(*And out through door*)
(*Street door*)

PORTER: Morning, Mr Mortimer.
MORTIMER (*tired*): Good morning, Tom.

> *(And out through door)*
> *(Street door)*

PORTER: Good morning, Mr Courtenay-Smith.
C.-SMITH (*vague*): Morning, Mr Thompson.

> *(And out through door)*
> *(Street door)*

PORTER: Good morning, Sir John.
SIR JOHN (*aloof*): Ah, Thompson . . .

> *(And out through door)*
> *(Street door)*

PORTER: Good morning, my Lord.
1ST LORD: Morning, Tommy. (*Conspiratorial*) Anything to report?
PORTER: All on schedule, my Lord.
1ST LORD: Jolly good.

> *(Through door)*

MYRTLE: Good morning, your Lordship.
1ST LORD: Good morning, Mrs Trelawney.

> *(Through door)*

MORTIMER: Good morning, my Lord.
1ST LORD: Good morning, ah, Mortimer.

> *(Through door)*

C.- SMITH: Good morning, Lord Coot.

1ST LORD: Good morning, Mr Courtenay-Smith.

(*Through door*)

SIR JOHN: What ho, Cooty.
1ST LORD: Morning, Jack.

(*Through door*)

BERYL: Good morning, sir.
1ST LORD (*startled*): Who are you?
BERYL: I'm new.

(*Pause*)

1ST LORD: I thought I couldn't account for you . . . New what?
BERYL: New secretary, sir . . . Miss Bligh. They sent me over from Directory Enquiries last night.
1ST LORD: I see. What happened to my old—to Miss—er—
BERYL: Apparently she cracked, sir, at 1.53 a.m. I came at once.
1ST LORD: That's the ticket. The Post Office never sleeps. Do you know the form round here?
BERYL: Well . . .
1ST LORD: Quite simple. I'm the First Lord of the Post Office, of course. I'm responsible for the lot, with special attention to the Telephone Services, which are as follows—write them down—
UMP—dial-the-Test-score.
SUN—dial-the-weather.
POP—dial-a-pop.
BET—dial-the-racing-results.
GOD—dial-the-Bible-reading.
EAT—dial-a-recipe.
And so on, with many others, including the most popular you see, we must keep a continuous check on all of them, because if you don't keep an eye on them they slide back.

The strain is appalling, and the staffing problems monumental.

Shall we start checking, then? To begin with, synchronize our watches, and then check with TIM—ready? I make it just coming up to nine two and forty seconds . . .

SCENE 3

Follows straight on with the Time signal (PIP PIP PIP).
  Heard direct, ie not through phone, as is GLADYS *now.*

GLADYS:

. . . At the third stroke it will be nine two and fifty seconds . . .
(PIP PIP PIP)
. . . At the third stroke it will be nine three precisely.
(PIP PIP PIP)

Or to put it another way, three minutes past nine, precisely, though which nine in particular, I don't say, so what's precise about that? . . .

. . . nine three and ten seconds . . .
(PIP PIP PIP)

The point is beginning to
  be lost on me.
Or rather it is becoming
  a different point.
Or rather I am beginning
  to see through it.
Because they think that
  time is something they
  invented,

for their own convenience,
and divided up into ticks
    and tocks
and sixties and twelves
and twenty-fours . . .
so that they'd know when
    the Olympic record
    has been broken
and when to stop serving
    dinner in second-class
    hotels,
when the season opens
    and the betting closes,
when to retire;
when to leave the station,
renew their applications
when their subscriptions
    have expired;
when time has run out.
So that they'd know how
    long they lasted,
and pretend that it
    matters,
and how long they've got,
as if it mattered,
so that they'd know that
    we know that they
    know.
That we know, that is.
That they know, of
    course.

And so on.

*(Faint time clock, 2-3
seconds)*

Ad infinitum.

I used to say ad nauseum
but it goes on long after
   you feel sick.
And I feel sick.
When you look down
   from a great height
you become dizzy. Such
   depth, such distance,
such disappearing tininess
so far away,
rushing away,
reducing the life-size to
   nothing—
it upsets the scale you
   live by.
Your eyes go first,
   followed by the head,
and if you can't look
   away you feel sick.
And that's my view of
   time;
and I can't look away.
Dizziness spirals up
   between my stomach
   and my head
corkscrewing out the
   stopper
But I'm empty anyway.
I was emptied long ago.

Because it goes on,
this endless dividing up
   into equal parts,
this keeping track—
because time viewed from
   such distance

etcetera
rushing away
reducing the lifespan to
   nothing
and so on—

(*Pause*)

The spirit goes first,
   followed by the mind.
And if you can't look
   away you go mad.

(*Time clock, 2-3 seconds*)

SCENE 4

FRANK *dialling; excited, intense. Ringing tone breaks off.*
OPERATOR *is heard through phone.*

OPERATOR: Number please.
FRANK: Listen, do all you people work in the same building?
OPERATOR: This is the operator—can I help you?
FRANK: I want to speak to Gladys Jenkins.
OPERATOR: What's the number, please?
FRANK: She works there—she's in the telephones, you see.
OPERATOR: Hello, sir—operator here—
FRANK: I want to be transferred to Mrs Jenkins—this is her
   husband.
OPERATOR: Mrs Jenkins?
FRANK: Speaking clock.
OPERATOR: Do you want to know the time?
FRANK: No—I want my Gladys! What's her number?
OPERATOR: Speaking clock?
FRANK: Yes.

OPERATOR: TIM
FRANK: Her *number*.
OPERATOR: T-I-M.
FRANK: I demand to speak to your superior—
OPERATOR: Just a moment, sir, putting you through.
GLADYS (*through phone*): . . . At the third stroke it will be nine twelve and forty seconds . . .
FRANK: It's all right, Glad—it's me again—Frank!

(GLADYS's *timespeak continues underneath*)

Can you hear me now, Glad?—I've had a time of it I can tell you—I must say, you gave me a turn! So that's where you got to—Gladys? Give over a minute, love—it's Frank—Can you hear me, Gladys? Give me a sign?

(*Pause; timeclock*)

I know your voice—it's you, isn't it Gladys—are they holding you?—I'll get you out of there, Gladys—I'll speak to the top man—I'll get the wheels turning, Gladys! I'll pull the strings, don't you worry, love—But I've got to dash now, love—I'm calling from the terminus and we're due out—

(IVY, *a bus conductress, breaks in*)

IVY: Frank *Jenkins*! The passengers are looking at their watches!
FRANK (*to* IVY): Just coming. (*To* GLADYS): That was Ivy, my conductress—you don't know Ivy—I'm on a new route now, the 52 to Acton—Keep your chin up, Glad—you can hear me can't you? I'll be giving you another ring later—Good-bye, Gladys—oh, Gladys—what's the time now?
GLADYS: Nine fourteen precisely—
FRANK: Thanks, Glad—oh, *thank* you, Gladys! (*He rings off*)
IVY (*off*): Frank—it's nine fourteen—remember the schedule!
FRANK (*going*): Hey, Ivy—I've found her—I've found my

Gladys!

SCENE 5

GLADYS (*direct voice now*):

. . . At the third stroke it
will be nine fourteen and
twenty seconds . . .
(PIP PIP PIP)

. . . At the third stroke . . .
I don't think I'll bother,
I don't think there's any
   point.
Let sleeping dogs and so
   on.
Because I wouldn't shake
it off by going back, I'd
only be in the middle of
   it,
with an inkling of infinity,
the only one who has
   seen both ends
rushing away from the
   middle.
You can't keep your
   balance after that.
Because they don't know
   what time is.
They haven't experienced
   the silence
in which it passes
impartial disinterested
   godlike.
Because they didn't invent
   it at all.

They only invented the
  clock.
And it doesn't go tick
and it doesn't go tock
and it doesn't go pip.
It doesn't go anything.
And it doesn't go
  anything for ever.
It just goes,
before them, after them,
without them,
above all without them,
and their dialling fingers,
their routine-checking,
  schedule-setting time-
  keeping clockwork—
luminous, anti-magnetic
fifteen-jewelled self-
winding, grandfather,
cuckoo, electric shock-,
dust- and waterproofed,
  chiming;
it counts for nothing
  against the scale of
  time,
and makes them tiny,
  bound and gagged to
  the minute-hand
as though across a railway
  line—
struggling without hope,
  eyes busy with silent-
  screen distress
as the hour approaches—
  the express
swings round the curve
  towards them

(and the Golden Labrador
   who might have saved
   them
never turns up on time).

                              (2-3 seconds)

And they count for
   nothing measured
   against
the moment in which a
   glacier forms and melts.
Which does not stop them
   from trying
to compete;
they synchronize their
   watches,
count the beats,
to get the most out of the
   little they've got,
clocking in, and out,
and speeding up,
keeping up with their
   time-tables,
and adjusting their tables
   to keep up with their
   speed,
and check one against
   the other
and congratulate each
   other—
a minute saved to make
   another minute possible
   somewhere else
to be spent another time.
Enough to soft-boil a third
   of an egg:

hard-boil a fifth.

Precisely . . .
(PIP PIP PIP)

(3-4 seconds)

Of course, it's a service if
    you like.
They dial for twenty
    second's worth of time
and hurry off contained
    within it
until the next correction,
with no sense of its
    enormity, none,
no sense of their scurrying
    insignificance;
only the authority of my
    voice,
the voice of the sun itself,
more accurate than
    Switzerland—
definitive
divine.

(2-3 seconds, very faint)

If it made a difference
I could refuse to play,
sabotage the whole illusion
a little every day if it
    made a difference,
as if it would, if I coughed
    or jumped a minute
(they'd correct their
    watches by my falter).
And if I stopped to

explain
At the third stroke it will
  be
too late to catch up, far
far too late, gentlemen . . .
they'd complain, to the
  Post Office
And if stopped altogether,
just stopped, gave up the
  pretence,
it would make no
  difference.
Silence is the sound of
  time passing.

At the third stroke it will
  be . . .
  *(Continues 3-4
  seconds)*

(1-2 seconds, faint)

Don't ask when the
  pendulum began to
  swing.
Because there is no
  pendulum.
It's only the clock that
  goes tick tock
and never the time that
  chimes.
It's never the time that
  stops.

(1-2 seconds, quick fade)

SCENE 6

VOICE THROUGH PHONE: . . . thirty minutes in a Regulo 5
oven until it is a honey coloured brown . . . Serves six.

1ST LORD (*ringing off*): Well, that's that one. Next.

BERYL: That was the last one, sir.

1ST LORD: Then start again at the beginning—continuous attention, you see. You'll have to take over this afternoon —I have a board meeting.

BERYL: Very good, sir.

1ST LORD: You don't have to call me sir. Call me my Lord.

BERYL: Very good, my Lord.

(*Phone rings*)

Hello?

FRANK (*through phone*): This is Frank Jenkins.

BERYL: Yes?

FRANK: It's about my wife.

BERYL: Yes?

FRANK: Is she there?

BERYL: This is the First Lord's office.

FRANK: I want the top man in speaking clocks.

BERYL: What name please?

FRANK: Jenkins—it's about my wife, Gladys. She's the speaking clock.

BERYL: Hold on, please.

My Lord, it's a Mr Jenkins—he says his wife is the speaking clock.

1ST LORD: How extraordinary. Tell him we don't know what he's talking about.

SCENE 7

GLADYS (*direct*):

. . . At the third stroke it will be eleven thirty precisely . . .
(PIP PIP PIP)

Old Frank . . .

Yes, we met dancing, I
    liked him from the first.
He said, 'If you're Glad
I'll be Frank . . .'
There was time to laugh
    then
but while I laughed a
    bumblebee
fluttered its wings a
    million times.
How can one compete?
His bus passed my window
    twice a day,
on the route he had then,
every day, with a toot and
    a wave and was gone.
toot toot toot
everything the same
if only you didn't know,
which I didn't
which I do.
He took his timetable
    seriously, Frank.
You could set your clock
    by him.
But not *time*—it flies by
unrepeatable
and the moment after
    next the passengers are
    dead
and the bus scrap and the
    scrap dust,
caught by the wind, blown
    into the crevasse
as the earth splits and
    scatters
at the speed of bees wings.

Old Frank. He had all
   the time
in the world for me,
such as it was.

(PIP PIP PIP)

SCENE 8

In the street FRANK's *bus comes to a rather abrupt halt, the
door of his cab opens, slams shut as he runs across the pave-
ment and through a door. He is breathless and in a frantic
hurry.*

FRANK: Hey, you—who's in charge here?

PORTER: I am. Is that your bus?

FRANK: Who's the top man—quick!

PORTER: You can't park there after seven if the months's got
an R in it or before nine if it hasn't except on Christmas
and the Chairman's birthday should it fall in Lent.

FRANK: I have an appointment with the chairman.

PORTER (*to the sound of horns*): Seems to be a bit of a traffic
jam out there.

FRANK: What floor's he on?

PORTER: He's not on the floor this early. Is this your conductress?

(*As the door flies open*)

IVY: Frank—what are you doing!

FRANK: All right, all right! (*To* PORTER) Listen—I'll be passing
your door again at one-fourteen. Tell him to be ready—

CONDUCTRESS: Frank—we'll get behind time!

FRANK (*leaving hurriedly*): It's all right, I got ninety seconds
ahead going round the park . . .

(*And out; and break*)

SCENE 9

In the street FRANK's *bus draws up once more; same slam, same feet, same door, same frenzy.*

FRANK: Where is he? I've got ninety-five seconds.
2ND PORTER: Who?
FRANK: Who are you?
2ND PORTER: What do you want?
FRANK: Where's the other porter?
2ND PORTER: Gone to lunch—it's one-fourteen.
FRANK: Never mind him—where's the chairman?
2ND PORTER: They eat together.

(*Door crashes open*)

CONDUCTRESS: Frank *Jenkins*!
2ND PORTER: Like brothers.
CONDUCTRESS: What about the schedule!?
FRANK (*to* PORTER): Listen—I'll be back here at two forty-seven—
CONDUCTRESS (*almost in tears*): I ask you to remember the schedule!
2ND PORTER (*as the horns sound*): Hello—is that your bus out there?
FRANK (*leaving hurriedly*): Two forty-seven!—tell him it's about Gladys Jenkins!

SCENE 10

GLADYS (*through phone*): . . . three fourteen and twenty

seconds . . .
  (PIP PIP PIP)
1ST LORD (*ringing off*): Precisely! Next!
BERYL: God, my Lord.
GOD (*though phone*): In the beginning was the Heaven and
  the Earth . . .

(Fade)

SCENE 11

GLADYS (*direct*):   . . . At the third stroke it
                                            will be three fourteen
                                            and fifty seconds . . .

Check, check, check . . .
One day I'll give him
    something
to check up for . . .
tick tock
tick tock
check check
chick chock
tick
you can check
your click clock
by my pip pip pip   (PIP PIP PIP)
I never waver,
I'm reliable,
lord, lord,
I'm your servant,
trained,
precisely.   . . . precisely.

  (With a click FRANK *is on the line)*
  (We hear him, as GLADYS *does, through the phone)*

FRANK: Hello, Gladys—it's Frank. I bet you wondered where I'd got to . . . Well, I've had a bit of trouble getting hold of the right man, you see, but don't you worry because the next trip will give me the time—I'll be bang outside his door slap in the middle of the rush hour so I'll have a good four minutes—can you hear me, Gladys? . . .

(*Breaks a little*)

Oh, Gladys—talk to me—I want you back, I'll let you do anything you like if you come back—I'll let you be a nun, if that's what you really want . . . Gladys? I love you, Gladys—
Hold on, love, hold on a bit, and I'll have you out of there . . .
Got to go now, Gladys, Ivy's calling me, we're due out. Bye bye . . . bye bye . . . (*Ring off*)

GLADYS:
I can hear them all
though they do not know enough to
speak to me.
I can hear them breathe,
pause, listen,
sometimes the frogsong of clockwindings
and the muttered repetition to the
nearest minute . . .
but never a question of a question,
never spoken,
it remains open, permanent,
demanding a different answer
every ten seconds.

Until Frank.
Oh, Frank, you knew my voice,
but how can I reply?
I'd bring the whole thing down with a cough,
stun them with a sigh . . .

(*Sobbing a little*)

I was going to be a nun, but they wouldn't have me because I didn't believe, I didn't believe *enough*, that is; most of it I believed all right, or was willing to believe, but not enough for their purposes, not about him being the son of God, for instance, that's the part that put paid to my ambition, that's where we didn't see eye to eye. No, that's one of the main points, she said, without that you might as well believe in a pair of old socks for all the good you are to us, or words to that effect. I asked her to stretch a point but she wasn't having any of it. I asked her to let me stay inside without being a proper nun, it made no difference to me, it was the serenity I was after, that and the clean linen, but she wasn't having any of that.

(*Almost a wail*)

But it's not the same thing at all!
I thought it would be—peace!
Oh, Frank—tell them—
I shan't go on, I'll let go
and sneeze the fear of God into
their alarm-setting, egg-timing,
train-catching, coffee-
   breaking faith in
an uncomprehended
   clockwork—

yes, if I let go,
lost track
changed the beat, went
   off the rails—
cracked—

                  . . . At the third stroke it
                  will be three eighteen
                  and ten seconds . . .

At the third stroke
it will be
three eighteen and
twenty seconds . . .
And so what?

At the third stroke
it will be
too late to do any good,
gentlemen—

At the third stroke
Manchester City 2,
Whores of Lancashire 43
    for seven declared
At the third stroke
Sheffield Wednesday will
    be cloudy
and so will Finisterre . . .
(*The Queen*) So a Merry
Christmas and God Bless
you everywhere . . .
And now the Prime
    Minister!:
Gentlemen, the jig is up
—I have given you
    tears . . .
And now the First Lord!—
Don't lose your heads
while all about you on
the burning deck . . .
Oh—Frank! Help me! . . .

(PIP PIP PIP)
At the third stroke
it will be
three eighteen and
twenty seconds . . .
(PIP PIP PIP)

At the third stroke
it will be
three eighteen and thirty
seconds . . .
(PIP PIP PIP)
At the third stroke . . .

SCENE 12

FRANK'S *bus stops abruptly. Same place, same slam, same feet, same door, same frenzy.*

FRANK: Right, let's not waste time—where is she?
PORTER: State your business.
FRANK: I'm looking for my wife.
PORTER: Name?
FRANK: Jenkins—you know me.
PORTER: *Her* name!
FRANK: Sorry—Jenkins.
PORTER: Better. Your name?
FRANK: Jenkins.
PORTER: Relative.
FRANK: Husband.
PORTER: Holds water so far.
FRANK: I demand to see your superior.
PORTER: Name?
FRANK: Jenkins!
PORTER: No one of that name here.
FRANK: I see your game—a conspiracy, is it?
PORTER (*as the horns sound*): Is that your bus out there?
FRANK: I demand to speak to the chief of speaking clocks.
PORTER (*as the door bursts open*): Here she comes.
IVY (*conductress*): I'm not covering up for you again, Frank Jenkins!
PORTER: Hey—you can't go in there!

(*Door*)

MYRTLE: Hello.
FRANK: Where's the top man?
MYRTLE: Keep on as you're going.

(*Door*)

MORTIMER: Who are you?

FRANK: I want my wife!

MORTIMER: Now, look here, old man, there's a time and place for everything—

FRANK: I want her back!

MORTIMER: My dear fellow, please don't make a scene in the office—

FRANK: You're holding her against her will—

MORTIMER: I think that's for her to say. The fact is that Myrtle and I are in love—

FRANK: I want my Gladys.

MORTIMER: Gladys? Isn't your name Trelawney?

FRANK: Jenkins—where's my Gladys?

MORTIMER: Gladys?

FRANK: My wife—

MORTIMER: Are you suggesting that a man of my scrupulous morality—

(*Door*)

MYRTLE: Darling, there's a bus conductress outside—

MORTIMER: Thank you, Mrs Trelawney—

IVY (*desperate*): Frank!—the traffic is beginning to move!

FRANK: I demand to see your superior!

MORTIMER: You can't go in there!

(*Door*)

C.-SMITH: Yes?

FRANK: Are you the top man?

MORTIMER: Excuse me, Mr Courtenay-Smith, this man just burst into—

IVY: Frank—I ask you to think of your schedule!

FRANK: Shut up! You there, are you the top man?

C.-SMITH: In my field, or do you speak hierarchically?

FRANK: I speak of Gladys Jenkins.

C.-SMITH: Not my field—

FRANK: You've got my wife—
MORTIMER: How dare you suggest that a man of Mr Courtenay-
Smith's scrupulous morality—
IVY: Frank! the passengers have noticed!

(*Door*)

C.-SMITH: Where's he gone?
MYRTLE: Darling, what's going on?
MORTIMER: Mrs Trelawney, I must ask you to address me—
C.-SMITH: My God—the time-and-motion system won't take
the strain!
IVY (*fading*): Fra-a-a-nk . . .!

SCENE 13

GLADYS (*breaking down slowly but surely*):
At the third stroke
I'm going to give it up,
yes, yes . . . it's asking
   too much,
for one person to be in
   the know
of so much, for so
   many . . .
and at the third stroke
Frank will come
. . . Frank . . .
I'm going to drop it now,
it can go on without me,
and it will,
time doesn't need me—
they think I'm time, but
   I'm not—
I'm Gladys Jenkins and

At the third stroke it
will be four twenty-
three and ten seconds . . .

at the third stroke
I'm going to cough,
sneeze
whisper an obscenity that
    will leave
ten thousand coronaries
    sprawled
across their telephone tables,
and the trains
    will run
    half empty
and all the bloody
    eggs will turn to
volcanic rock smoking
    in dry cracked
    saucepans
as soon as I shout—
Ship!
(a vessel)
*Pis*cine!
(pertaining to fishes)
*Fruc!*tuate
(fruit-bearing)

(*She giggles
hysterically*)

oh yes I will
and then they'll let me go
they'll have to
because Frank knows I'm
    here—
come on, please Frank, I
    love you
and at the third stroke I
    will
yes I will at the third

stroke I will . . .

SCENE 14

1ST LORD: Well, gentlemen, in bringing this board meeting to a close, and I'm sure you're all as bored as I am,

(*Chuckle chuckle, hear hear*)

I think we must congratulate ourselves on the variety and consistency of the services which we in the telephone office have maintained for the public in the face of the most difficult problems. I believe I'm right in saying that if the last Test Match had not been abandoned because of the rain, UMP would barely have lasted the five days, but all was well as it happened, though the same rainy conditions did put an extra strain on SUN our weather forecast service . . . I don't know if you have anything to add, Sir John?

SIR JOHN: Well, Cooty—my Lord, that is—only to join with the rest of the Board in heartily congratulating you on the excellent report—

(*Hear hear hear hear*)

1ST LORD: Thank you. Now is there any other business?

(*Door*)

FRANK (*out of breath*): Where's Gladys Jenkins?!
1ST LORD: There you have me, gentlemen.
SIR JOHN: Point of order, my Lord.
1ST LORD: Yes, Jack?
SIR JOHN: I don't think this man—
FRANK: I'm not taking any more of this—where've you got

my Glad—

(*Door*)

C.-SMITH: Forgive me, my Lord—this man is quite unauthorized—
IVY: Frank, the passengers are rioting! All is lost!
MORTIMER: Now look here—
MYRTLE: Darling, do shut up!
FRANK: Damn you. What have you done with my wife?
SIR JOHN: Don't you come here with your nasty little innuendos, Trelawney—whatever you may have heard about the Bournemouth conference, Myrtle and I—
IVY: The passengers are coming!

> (FIRST LORD *gets quiet by banging his gavel*)
> (*Pause*)
> (*Noise of rioting passengers*)

1ST LORD: Gentlemen—please! (*Pause*) Now what's all the row about?
IVY: It's the passengers, sir.
FRANK: Are you the top man?
1ST LORD: Certainly.
FRANK: What have you done with my Gladys?
MORTIMER: How dare you suggest that a man of the First Lord's scrupulous morality—
1ST LORD: Please, Mr Mortimer, let him finish.
FRANK: She's the speaking clock.
1ST LORD: What do you mean? *TIM?*
FRANK: Gladys. Yes.
1ST LORD (*chuckling*): My dear fellow—there's no Gladys—we wouldn't trust your wife with the *time*—it's a machine, I thought everyone knew that . . .
FRANK: A machine?
1ST LORD: He thought it was his wife!

> (*General chuckles*)

Wife . . . thought it was his wife! . . .

FRANK: It was her voice—

IVY: Oh, Frank—they wouldn't use your Glad for that. It's just the speaking clock—

FRANK: She was educated—

IVY: Oh Frank—come on, come on now, we'll be in awful trouble with the Inspector.

FRANK: But Ivy—she *talked* to me . . .

IVY: She couldn't have done—

1ST LORD: She *talked* to you, my dear fellow?

FRANK: Well, not exactly . . .

IVY: Of course she didn't. Come on, now . . .

1ST LORD: That's it—back to your offices gentlemen. We must all make up for lost time.

(*General movement out*)

FRANK: But she sounded like my Gladys . . .

IVY: You'll have to go on looking, Frank . . .

(FIRST LORD *alone*)

1ST LORD: Dear me, dear me . . .

(*Door*)

BERYL (*urgent*): Sir!

1ST LORD: What is it, Miss Bligh?

BERYL: It's the speaking clock—I was just checking it and—

1ST LORD: All right—get me TIM, I'll see to it.

BERYL: Yes, my Lord. (*Dialling*) She's on now, my Lord.

GLADYS (*through phone. Sobbing hysterically*): At the third stroke it will be five thirty five and fifty seconds . . .
(PIP PIP PIP)

1ST LORD: Mrs Jenkins . . . This is the First Lord speaking.

GLADYS: At the third stroke it will be five thirty-six precisely . . .

1ST LORD: Mrs Jenkins—pull yourself together, stop crying.

And you've lost forty seconds somewhere by my watch—

GLADYS: At the third stroke I don't know what time it is and don't care, because it doesn't go tick tock at all, it just goes and I have seen—I have seen infinity!

1ST LORD: *Mrs Jenkins!*

GLADYS (*sniffing*): I can't go on!

1ST LORD: Come on now, this isn't like you at all. Let's get things back on the rails, hm? Think of the public, Mrs Jenkins . . . Come on now . . . at the third stroke . . .

GLADYS: At the third stroke . . .

1ST LORD: It will be five thirty-seven and forty seconds.

(PIP PIP PIP)

Carry on from there . . .

GLADYS: At the third stroke it will be five thirty-seven and fifty seconds . . .

1ST LORD: That's it—spot on Mrs Jenkins. Control your voice now.

(PIP PIP PIP)

GLADYS: At the third stroke it will be five thirty-eight precisely.

1ST LORD: Well done, Mrs Jenkins. Well done—I'll check you again within the hour, as usual. (*Rings off*)

GLADYS (*direct now*):   At the third stroke it
                                      will be five thirty-eight
                                      and ten seconds . . .

He thinks he's God . . .   (PIP PIP PIP)
                                      At the third stroke . . .

(*Fading out*)

ON A DAY IN SUMMER IN A GARDEN

Don Hawarth

Characters

DICK

JIM

JACK

ON A DAY IN SUMMER IN A GARDEN

Birds: A dawn chorus.

DICK: Nice morning.
JIM: Grand.

> *(Bullocks low and sheep bleat in the distance. Birds near and far dive and tweet. The conversation is leisurely. These country sounds are heard behind it and during the quite long pauses)*

JIM: Nippy though.
DICK: Morning mist. Morning mist and morning dew. Going to be hot today, young Jack.
JACK: Is it, grandad?
DICK: When the sun strikes through on a hot day, early summer, there's no better thing in creation than to be a dock plant in this garden.
JIM: Because we fear nothing.
DICK: Correct.
JACK: What is there to fear, uncle Jim?
DICK ⎱ : Nothing.
JIM ⎰ : Encroachment.
JACK: What's encroachment, uncle Jim?
JIM: The other plants encroaching.
DICK: But we don't fear it.
JIM: Attempting to choke us.
DICK: Because we're more than equal.
JIM: Sometimes.
DICK: Always, Jim.
JIM: Not always, Dick. A large number of dock plants have been lost through the years.
DICK: You're here, I'm here, young Jack's here. This is our patch of the garden.
JIM: We've tried to teach them that.
DICK: Well then, it's finally sunk in.

JIM (*laughs*): I don't think those daisies will come again.

JACK: What's daisies?

DICK: Surface leaf, white flower, close up at night. We throttled them.

JIM: Choked their life out.

DICK: And before that the charlock.

JIM: And before that the cornflower.

DICK: And before that the hoary pepperwort.

JIM: Forget-me-not.

DICK: Nettle annual.

JIM: Bramble.

DICK: Wild turnip and shepherds needle.

JIM: Pennycress and sowthistle.

DICK: The creeping buttercup.

JIM: The deadly nightshade.

DICK: And was the poppy before that?

JIM: And when was the groundsel?

DICK: And the tares and the dandelions.

JIM: And the thistles and treacle mustard.

DICK: It's hard to remember which came in what year. We've choked them all in our time.

(*Pause—country sounds*)

JACK: Grandad, are there years when other plants don't encroach?

DICK: Many.

JACK: Then you must be very old grandad, you and uncle Jim.

JIM: Been here since this garden began.

JACK: And what was before that, uncle Jim?

JIM: That was the beginning, I suppose, the first season ever.

JACK: But before that.

JIM: There could be nothing before that, could there, Dick?

DICK: I've forgotten, Jim. It's not quite so straightforward. I did have an explanation of it once.

(*Pause—country sounds*)

JACK: Grandad.

DICK: Son?

JACK: I hope they don't encroach this year.

DICK: No.

JACK: The other plants.

DICK: They won't. And what if they do? We're firmly rooted.

JIM: We've got a good grip.

DICK: Tenacious. Steadfast.

JIM: We've got our tap roots down, knotted round the limestone.

JACK: But I haven't, uncle Jim, not limestone, only soil. They might—

DICK: They won't, Jackie. (*aside*) Why did you have to mention that?

JIM (*aside*): I didn't think.

DICK (*aside*): Rattling the young chap.

JACK (*in alarm*): The other plants, they could encroach on me. They'll have me up, whisk me out.

DICK: Not remotely. You're with us. Me and your uncle Jim have defeated all encroachers from the beginning of time. And we're ready, aren't we, Jim?

JIM: Yes.

DICK: To give a repeat performance.

JIM: Yes.

DICK: Any season, upon any plant, herb, weed or growth of any pestiferous species whatsoever that has the audacity, the temerity, the utter crass and reckless folly to invade our patch of the garden.

    (JACK *laughs reassured*)

DICK: So there. (*He laughs briefly, pauses, then lets out a sigh, long and contented*) Aahhhh. A grand feeling, the mist dispersed and the sun warming the dew from your fronds. Ohhhh it's grand to be alive.

    (*A buzz of bees. Birds close. Sheep and bullocks in the distance. Fade. Silence*)

JIM (*alarmed*): What was that?

DICK: What?

JIM: Noise.

DICK: What noise?

JIM (*alarmed*): It was his tank.

JACK (*alarmed*): What's a tank, uncle Jim?

JIM: A tank, his spraying tank.

JACK: What's a spraying tank, grandad?

DICK (*calmly*): Nothing. Something the persons have.

JACK: What for?

DICK: Spraying.

JACK: What's spraying?

DICK: A kind of rain.

JACK (*relieved*): Rain's all right.

JIM: In moderation.

DICK (*affably*): Your uncle Jim doesn't like it. That's why he grows up the wall side.

JIM: It suits me.

DICK: You're dusty, Jim.

JIM: No.

DICK (*bantering*): Grubby. You could do with a clean up. If he spots you (*laughing*) he'll let you have it with the spray.

JIM: Now that's not a joke, that's not funny, that's not in good taste.

JACK: What *is* the spray?

JIM: It's what he brings and—

DICK: All right, Jim, all right.

JACK: But what is it, grandad?

DICK: Like I said, like rain. ˙

JIM: You're bringing the lad up on lies.

DICK: I'm bringing him up to be intrepid.

JIM (*ridiculing*): Intrepid.

DICK: Yes, intrepid. Not cowering against the wallside for fear of the rain.

JIM: I've seen you miserable enough in the rain, Dick, sodden there and drooping.

DICK: Nonsense. You're dusty, Jim, from cowering against that wall. You're assymetric.

JACK (*making the peace*): But he's quite tall, grandad.

JIM: Considerably taller than your grandad.

DICK: He's got next to no leaf.

JIM (*ironically*): And your grandad, Jack, has some lovely broad fronds.

DICK: I do at least look like a dock plant, not crawling up the wallside like the nettles.

JIM (*laughs, ridiculing*): You look like a clump of rhubarb.

DICK (*angry*): I what? I what?

JACK (*distressed*): Uncle Jim. Grandad, please—

DICK: All right, Jack. (*Pause*) Let's not spoil a nice day. I apologise, Jim.

JIM (*after a pause*): All right. (*Pause—then by way of explanation*) I'm dusty because the wind twists up the loose soil and tosses it against the wall. Can't help it.

DICK: Understood, Jim.

(*He pauses, waiting for Jim to speak, then, as Jim doesn't speak—*)

And as to *your* allusion?

JIM: Allusion?

DICK: Comparison?

JIM: Comparison?

DICK: Of me to—you know.

JIM: Do I—what?

JACK (*whispers*): Rhubarb, uncle Jim.

JIM: Oh yes. I withdraw, Dick. You don't resemble a clump of rhubarb.

(*Country sounds. Fade. The voices of the man and woman are at a distance*)

WOMAN (*asking a question*): Hebble trebble babble settle?

MAN (*replying*): Base trough rough rass.

WOMAN: Hebble trebble ten.
MAN: Base trough.
JIM: He's going to the field.

(*Clang of a gate closing*)

JACK: Grandad.
DICK: Hm. Hm.
JACK: The noises the persons make—are they talking?
DICK: I suppose, in a way.
JIM: Communicating.
DICK: In a general sort of way.
JIM: Same as the animals. The bullocks low and the sheep
    bleat—I suppose there are different ways of lowing and
    bleating, Dick, and each will express something different.
DICK: Simple things, I suppose, Jim—anger, warning, things
    like that. Contentment.

(*A distant bullock lows long and contented*)

    All animals can convey what they feel to some extent.
JIM: But not actually converse.
DICK: No.
JIM: Not hold a conversation.
DICK: Not an intelligent conversation.
JIM: Like us.
JACK: And the persons, grandad?
DICK: Much the same, I suppose.
JIM: Communicating.
DICK: But nothing precise. The bullocks low and the sheep
    bleat and the persons, one of them babbles and one
    burbles.
JACK: Why are there two, grandad?
DICK: Everything comes in numbers. There's three of us here.
JIM: And there used to be many more.
JACK: What happened to—
DICK (*overriding the question*): And there's a number of docks

by the pond and all that mob over there.

JIM: Common lot. They tolerate anything there. There's some curly leaf docks amongst that lot.

JACK: What are curly leaf docks, uncle Jim?

JIM: Foreigners, riff-raff. Blown in from miles away.

DICK: The older persons that once lived in the house used to tip tins amongst them. They'd perform undignified tricks like growing through the bottom.

JIM: Common lot.

JACK: What happened to the older persons?

DICK: Taken away in a vehicle.

JACK: Why?

DICK: I can't say, Jack.

JIM: Well the persons when they're dead don't rot down like plants, do they?

DICK: Is that it? That sounds a very likely explanation, Jim.

JACK: What's 'dead', grandad? What's 'rotting down'?

JIM: Docks rot down when they're dead.

JACK: Will I be dead? Will I rot down?

DICK: No. Get a firm grip with your tap roots, Jackie. Be tenacious. They'll never shift you.

JIM: They've come at us with all sorts of things in our time.

DICK: The sickle. Lopped us with the sickle.

JIM: And uprooting.

DICK: Spade, fork and the other thing.

JIM: The pick.

DICK: That's right. The pick. Came at us baldheaded with the pick. Stones, worms, soil, insects, everything tossed into the air and the old person tugging at us with the pick, bellowing imprecations, wasn't he, Jim (*Jim agrees*) with the dew running off him and a stinking mist enveloping him.

JIM: He gave off the most noisome exhalation, the older person.

DICK: He collapsed.

JIM: He did. Something in him cracked.

DICK: And they took him off in the vehicle.

JACK: Will they come at me with the pick?

DICK: No. No. Get your tap roots down, then no matter how

much they tug and snap you, you're there again next spring.

JIM: To salute the season.

DICK: Precisely.

JACK: But when they snap you, you've lost the sky and the birds and the trees and the bullocks.

DICK: You have, you have. You're in the darkness of the soil. You've missed a bit of summer. It's like an early onset of the winter.

JIM: Except the soil is still warm.

DICK: That's so.

JIM: And it feels odd. Quite odd. We've experienced it a number of times, haven't we, Dick?

DICK: We have, at their hands.

(*Sound of sheep, bullocks and birds. Fade*)

JACK: Grandad.

DICK (*sleepy*): Hm, hm.

JACK: The persons.

DICK: Hm, hm.

JACK: Why do they live in the house?

DICK: I've never thought.

JIM: It's to make the little ones grow fast.

DICK: Is it, Jim?

JIM: Yes, like the plants in the glass frame.

DICK: Plants in the glass frame grow whitish instead of green.

JIM: And the little people, all whitish. The house forces their growth.

DICK: Very unhealthy.

JIM: And it's said they stay above ground all winter.

DICK: That can't possibly be healthy.

JIM: Remember when we went into the house, Dick?

DICK: I do.

JACK: Into the house?

JIM: Us and the other plants.

DICK: The persons had gone away.

JIM: In through the window frames and the cracks in the walls.

DICK: The nettles did well.

JIM (*deprecating*): For nettles.

DICK: Clumps of them growing inside the house.

JIM: And bindweed. And the grasses perched on high ledges.

DICK: And do you remember that dock, Jim—what was his name—growing out of the top of the chimney pot?

JIM: I do. And all of the docks pressing against the window panes from the inside.

DICK: We shall take possession again. We'll drive the persons out. We'll shove into every crevice. We'll topple the house down, oh yes.

JACK: Why grandad? Why should we want to do that?

DICK: Eh? I've never really thought. It's self-evidently desirable wouldn't you say, Jim?

JIM: Oh yes, a much more natural state of affairs.

DICK: Quite so. Quite so.

(*Country sounds. Fade. Clang of gate*)

JIM: He's back.

MAN (*calling*): O-pal.

WOMAN: Treble boff hip.

MAN: O yump wippy tip.

WOMAN: Deep tip in bode.

MAN: Yump hen.

(*Door closes*)

JACK: Grandad. The persons *are* two.

DICK: I've explained. Things come in numbers.

JIM: But persons *are* two, Dick. The old persons, two, and these persons, two.

DICK: Yes. Now I do remember something—

JIM: It's perhaps—

DICK: Just let me think. (*Pause*) It's something to do with them not going to seed.

JIM (*puzzled*): That there are two?

DICK: Yes, that there has to be two.
JIM: How?
DICK: I can't quite remember. I did have an explanation of it once.

(*Country sounds, then: a bluster of wind. A loud cushioned fall*)

(*Dick laughs*) Caterpillar.
JIM: Where? Where's it landed?
DICK (*laughs*): On you.

(JACK *joins in Dick's laughter*)

DICK: Breeze blew it out of the tree.
JIM: Where on me, where?
DICK: You'll know when he starts his dinner.

(DICK *and* JACK *laugh*)

DICK: Listen.

(*A slow, heavy crunching sound which continues*)

(DICK *and* JACK *laugh*)

JACK: Where is he, grandad?
JIM (*indignant, not alarmed*): Get off. Get off.
DICK: On your uncle Jim's top frond.
JIM: Get off. Get off.

(DICK *and* JACK *laugh*)

DICK: Look up, Jackie. Can you see where he's gnawing through?
JACK (*laughs with delight*): A patch, a light green patch. It's growing lighter still.

JIM: Get off. Go back where you came from.

JACK (*excited*): It's eaten through. There's a hole, grandad. I can see the sky and the clouds.

DICK: It'll be a dry, dusty dinner for Mr Caterpillar. He'll have a thirsty afternoon.

JIM: That's uncalled for. Get off. Get off.

(*A bluster of wind*)

That's shifted him.

JACK: Where's he gone?

JIM: Blown somewhere.

(*The slow heavy crunching is heard again*)

(JIM *laughs*)

JACK (*happily*): What is it, uncle Jim? What is it?

JIM (*laughs*): He's landed (*he laughs*) on your grandfather.

(JIM *and* JACK *laugh*)

DICK: All right. All right.

JIM: He'll get a sloppier dinner now.

DICK (*laughing a little*): All right, all right, all right.

(JIM *and* JACK *laugh and* DICK, *despite himself, joins in. The crunching sound fades under their laughter which continues merrily until* JIM *cuts it short*)

JIM (*alarmed*): What was that?

DICK: What?

JIM: It was his tank, wasn't it, the spraying tank.

DICK: It wasn't. He's going to the field again.

(*Gate clangs closed*)

JACK: Grandad, if it had been the spraying tank—

DICK: It wasn't.

JACK: But if it had been.

DICK: We should have remained unaffected. Your uncle Jim's gone as soft as an elder bush growing against that wall.

JACK: But what is the spray?

JIM: A leprous distillment. A poisonous and pestiferous exhalation. A noxious and deadly cloud.

DICK: Rarely encountered. Rarely encountered.

JIM: An ever-present threat.

DICK: Everything's an ever-present threat, Jim. Life is lived in ever-present threats.

JACK (*anxiously*): But if the spray is noxiferous, grandad—

DICK: The spray is nothing. (*Diverting him*) The creeping buttercup, now then, to me that's far more insidious.

JACK: And more noxiferous?

DICK: By far. You don't see it coming. Do you remember when we didn't see it coming, Jim?

JIM (*sulkily*): Hm.

JACK: But how does it arrive, grandad, if you don't see it coming?

DICK: Insidiously, that's the point. Pushes out green creepers and flat leaves, lying below sight and choking the life out of the grasses and plants as it approaches. Nothing to see, then suddenly they've arrived, yellow all along the horizon, the flower heads.

(JACK *shrieks*)

Brilliant yellow. Brighter than the sun. You could be blinded and paralysed and it's exactly then that you've got to remember it's not the flower heads that kill, it's the creepers and the flat green leaves, and the moment you can see the flower heads it's almost too late because the creepers operate forward of them. They could finish you while you're staring aghast at the nodding flowers.

(JACK *makes an appalled and fearful sound*)

JIM: Dick, if you wanted to scare the lad stiff, you've succeeded.

JACK: Have they come at you like that, grandad?

DICK: They have and this is the point: we're still here. I'm not alarming him, Jim, I'm teaching him life's lesson. I want him to grow up intrepid.

JACK: I don't know whether I'll ever be that, grandad.

DICK: You will. At times like that, when the creeping buttercup comes, remain calm, rely on your tap roots. Be tenacious. Stand your ground. They came. They've gone. We remain.

JIM: Some of the other docks—

DICK: What others?

JIM: A whole patch of others.

DICK: No, docks are perennial. Docks are indestructible.

JIM: It's not the same thing.

JACK: But there must have been others, grandad.

DICK } : How?
JACK { : Of course.

JACK: When the docks took possession of the house and grew out of the chimney pots. There must have been many growing then that are not here now.

DICK: Well, yes. (*Pause*) It's quite true, the house became reinfested.

JACK: What's that mean, grandad?

DICK: The persons came back.

JIM: And drove the plants out.

JACK: What happened to the plants?

DICK: I don't know, Jack. (*Pause*) It's just that sometimes the spring arrives and a plant you've known for many years doesn't come up again.

JACK (*reflective and serious*): I see.

(*Birds, bees and distant country sounds are heard*)

DICK (*more brightly*): But then sometimes a summer breeze springs up like the breeze that's blowing now and whisks a seed from the stem of a dock plant and drops it in the warm soil.

JACK: Does it?

DICK: Then the next spring, though some of the old ones might not arise again, you find to your utter surprise a young 'un growing, like yourself.

JACK (*laughs with a thrill of pleasure*): Like me.

(JACK *laughs.* DICK *and* JIM *laugh*)

JIM: So there, young Jack.

JACK: I'm glad I'm here with you, grandad, and uncle Jim.

DICK: And so are we.

JIM: There were some cantankerous knotted old plants. It was time we had new growth.

DICK: Like Jack.

JIM (*congratulatory*): Exactly like Jack. (JACK *laughs self-consciously with pleasure*)

(*Pause—distant country sounds. Birds*)

JACK: Grandad?

DICK: Jack.

JACK: Next spring, you will come up again?

DICK: Of course.

JACK: And you, uncle Jim?

JIM: Every time.

JACK: We'll always come up, won't we, all of us every spring.

DICK: Of course. We're perennial.

(*Distant sheep, bullocks, birds, closer the wind blusters, then the gate clangs*)

DICK: Back from the field. Too breezy for him.

JACK: Grandad.

DICK: Son?

JACK: Grandad, the persons move and the buttercups creep and we—well, we're rooted, aren't we?

DICK: We are indeed. Steadfast.

JACK: Why do the persons move?

JIM: It's to get out of the way of the bullocks.

DICK: I never heard that, Jim.

JIM: Yes. The docks in the field, the bullocks bogged on them.

DICK: They did, last summer.

JIM: Flattened them under a right sloppy load.

JACK: Is that more dangerous than the creeping buttercup, uncle Jim?

JIM: By no means. It's merely unpleasant, caked with dung, and dust accumulating and flies buzzing round.

DICK: Distasteful more than anything.

JIM: Yes, distasteful.

JACK: I was asking about the persons moving.

JIM: That's the explanation. They move so they don't get bogged on by the bullocks.

JACK: But the bullocks can move too, uncle Jim.

JIM: Yes.

JACK: So that if the persons move the bullocks can also move and bog on them where they've moved to.

DICK: That's right, Jim.

JIM: Perhaps. It doesn't seem to work out like that in practice.

JACK: Perhaps that's why he closes the gate.

JIM: How?

JACK: So the bullocks can't follow into the house and bog on him there.

(*Distant lowing of bullocks. Sheep, birds*)

JIM (*suddenly and alarmed*): Now that was the tank, that was his tank. Listen.

(*Sound of tap water drumming into container*)

DICK: He can't spray today, not with this breeze blowing.

JIM: Is it blowing? It's dropped.

DICK: Of course it's blowing, it blew the caterpillar. You miss half the happenings of life under the shelter of that wall.

JACK: Why can't he spray if it's blowing?

DICK: It'd blow the spray over him. He'd go orange and purple and mottled. He'd crack like a rotten stick.

JACK (*alarmed*): Is that what happens when you're sprayed, grandad?

JIM (*frightened*): Yes, it is.

DICK: And quite apart from the breeze, it's clouded over. It's going to rain. He can't spray today.

(*Door closed*)

JIM (*frightened but ironic*): He doesn't seem to have your grasp of the subject, Dick. He's about to commence.

(*Distant clank of the tank*)

DICK: Where is he?

JIM: Over there, at the far wall.

(*Hiss of spray at some distance*)

(*In panic*) O-O-O. O-O-O. O, I can't go through that again.

JACK (*in panic*): Again?

JIM: Every year.

DICK (*loudly*): Pull yourself together, Jim. Two seasons, three seasons, what are ten seasons? They'll tire and we'll not tire and we'll be into the house again next year or the year after or in a thousand years.

JIM: We shan't see a thousand years. We shan't see the autumn.

(JACK *starts to wail*)

DICK: Jack.

JACK: Grandad, I don't want to go orange and purple.

DICK: You won't, son.

JACK: I don't want to go mottled. I don't want to crack like a rotten stick. I don't want to wither and rot down and die. You promised we'd all be here again in spring.

DICK: We will.

JACK: I've seen nothing, grandad. I've never known an autumn. I was looking forward to what you said once, a snug winter in the soil.

DICK: And you shall have it, lad.

JIM: You said that last summer to Tom.

JACK: Tom?

JIM: And Henry.

JACK: Henry?

JIM: And Bill and John and Joseph, and Tony and Alfred and Robert in the couch grass, and Stanley and Eric and Archie and Fred by the footpath, and Jack and Arthur and Martin and Roy and Peter and Graham and Philip and Dennis.

(*During this roll-call Dick, trying to calm and quieten him, keeps saying—*)

DICK: All right. All right. All right.

(JIM *exhausts his list with a weary groan and* JACK *wails*)

DICK: Jack, he's old and hysterical and silly. Now listen. When there's danger some succumb and some survive, and you and I will survive. And Jim, despite his lack of character will also survive.

JACK: But grandad, how can you tell?

JIM: He can't tell. They wouldn't even need to take the spray to you, nipper. They'd whisk you up with the hoe.

(JACK *wails*)

DICK: That is rotten, Jim, that really is rotten.

JIM: But truthful. They threw your intrepid in your face last year when they were swelling and writhing and their roots twisting up through the cracking soil.

(JACK *wails with greater force*)

DICK: Jack.

(JACK *continues to wail*)

DICK (*sharply*): Jack!

(JACK *stops*)

DICK (*confidently*): He is not going to come here today.

(JIM *gives a bitter and hollow laugh*)

DICK: He is not going to come here for two reasons, first, that the breeze being where it is he can't spray into this wall side without getting the spray back over himself. Second, that even if he could we're too small a clump to catch his eye.

JIM (*bitterly and mournfully*): We are now.

DICK: And a third reason, now just be quiet a moment and feel. (*Pause*) What do you feel?

JACK: Frightened, grandad.

DICK: No, on your fronds, what do you feel?

JACK: Moisture, grandad? Moisture?

DICK: It's starting to rain.

(DICK *laughs*)

JIM: It's not.

DICK (*laughs with an assumed confidence*): Rain is coming.

JIM (*in the calm tone of terror*): I can see what it is that's coming.

(*Pump and hiss of spray*)

JACK: Where is he? Where is he?

JIM: On the far side, by the pond, advancing behind that silver cloud.

DICK (*amazed*): It's rolling back off the wall. The breeze is blustering the fumes round his head. He can't go on like this much longer.

JIM: Plants are perishing already.

DICK: The rain'll come and swill it off.

JIM: It won't rain today—it's too windy.

DICK: All right then, windy. Unsuitable for spraying. If he knew his business—

JIM: But he doesn't, Dick. That's why we're all going to catch it today.

(*Pump and hiss of spray*)

JACK: Grandad, if the noxiferous cloud envelopes me—

DICK: Noxious or pestiferous, Jackie, those are the correct words.

JIM: Meaning lethal.

DICK: Meaning unpleasant, highly unpleasant. The buttercup is worse and the bramble is worse, to say nothing of being bogged on by the bullocks.

JACK: But grandad—

DICK: Shhh. Listen.

(*Pause. Only the distant country sounds are heard*)

JACK: He's stopped. He's gone.

DICK: Yes.

JACK: He *has* stopped, uncle Jim.

JIM: Quiet. Listen . . . Yes, he has.

DICK (*laughs*): Too windy, rain hanging about, should never have commenced.

JACK (*laughs*): I was frightened, uncle Jim.

JIM: Me too, I don't mind admitting it. I'm not as young as I was.

DICK: Quite so. But try and be calmer, Jim. It must be harmful to your constitution to get worked up like that.

JIM: I haven't been too well this season.

DICK (*sympathetically*): No.

JIM: I wasn't always in a state.

DICK: No, you weren't, Jim.

JACK: I hope I grow up intrepid like you, grandad.

DICK: You will, son, have no fear . . . Ah well, not a bad afternoon. Bit chillier though as the day wears on. (*He laughs*) Uncle Jim's nodding off.

(JACK *laughs.* DICK *silences him*)

DICK: Shhh.

(JACK *gives a little pleased chuckle*)

JACK (*quietly and with affection and admiration*): Grandad.

DICK (*quietly and warmly returning the affection*): All right, Jack lad?

JACK (*laughs*): All right.

DICK (*with exhaustion and contentment*): Ahhhh.

(*Distant country sounds and birds near and far are heard and held.*
Suddenly the pump and hiss of the spray)

(JIM *wakes up with a tremor of terror*)

JIM: Oo-oo. Ah-ah-ah.

JACK: Grandad! Grandad!

DICK (*roused*): Umph?

JACK: It's started. He's spraying again.

JIM: Oo-oo. Ah-ah-ah.

DICK: Jim, pull yourself together. Where is he?

JIM: Oo-oo.

DICK (*insistently*): Where is he, Jim?

JIM: Over there. Advancing on that big clump.

DICK: Which big clump?

JIM: The ones with the tins and the curly dock amongst them. He's letting them have it now.

> (*From the distance of the clump: pump and hiss of spray. Drumming patter of falling droplets, like rain on canvas.*
> *From the attacked clump of docks a crowd shout: protest, indignation, abuse, stream of insults, threats, orders to clear off in vulgar terms*)

DICK: Common lot that.

> (*From the distance of the clump: pump, hiss and fall of droplets. Further shouts from crowd. The sounds of the spraying (pump, hiss and fall) competes with the shouting of the crowd. The shouting grows hoarse but at a high volume*)

JIM (*timorously*): He's got 'em.

> (*From the distance of the clump: the sound of the spraying continues as the shouting becomes hoarse and panting*)

JIM: They're rising up in the sky like contorted worms, they're swelling like melons.

JACK: Oh, grandad.

> (*From the distance of the clump: the last hoarse cries of anger and hatred turn to strangled moaning. The spraying stops. The crowd moaning becomes feebler. A separate*

sudden shout of agony)

JIM: Look at that, that chap writhing up, his head purple and orange and—oh, it's burst open.

(*Distant: sharp cry, then feeble mass moaning which fades under the dialogue*)

JACK (*whimpering*): Grandad, they *have* turned orange and purple. They *have* swelled and reared up and burst apart.
DICK: He'll turn orange and purple. He'll burst apart. It's blowing all over him.
JACK (*pleading in fear*): Grandad, please grandad.
DICK: He'll not come here, Jack.
JIM (*mocking*): Because we're too small a clump. Look what he's taking aim at now. A solitary plant.

(*Pump, hiss and fall of spray*)
(JACK *wails*)

DICK: It's all right, it's commencing to rain. The rain'll swill it off. Just a bit of burning, that's all.
JIM: Tell that clump over there it's commencing to rain. They'd like to hear it's commencing to rain.

(*Distant and low hoarse groans, final expiring gasps. A moment of silence*)

JIM (*in panic*): Ah-ah-ah. He's coming, he's coming, he's coming. This is it now.
DICK: Steady, Jack lad.

(*Boots approach through grass and stop.
Pause: distant country sounds heard*)

MAN (*close*): Bubble stubble runt beg.
WOMAN (*distant*): Be tinketer fister wobble.

MAN (*close*): Yump hen.

> (*His boots go away*)
> (DICK *lets out a long sigh*)

DICK: Close shave.
JACK (*weary with fear and relief*): Oh, grandad.
JIM: He'll come back. He's gone to refill his tank.
DICK: He's gone to die. It was blowing all over him.
JIM: He'll come back.
DICK: Not now, it's raining.
JIM: It's not raining.
DICK: It's hanging about. It's in the atmosphere.
JIM: There's only one thing I can see in the atmosphere.
JACK: What, uncle Jim?
JIM: The tap roots of that big clump over there.

> (JACK *makes weak sounds of distress*)

DICK: They were rabble. They got preoccupied with growing through tins. They didn't get their tap roots down. When he comes at you with the spray you need character, tenacity.
JACK: But will he come back, grandad?
DICK: Yes, he will sometime, Jackie. Not necessarily today, not this year perhaps, but sometime, and then you've simply got to hold on. Be tenacious. It's them or us, and if we're steadfast we'll see them all die and taken off in the vehicle and one day, perhaps a very distant day when you're as old as me and uncle Jim are now, we'll be back into the house and eventually—and you may live to see it— we'll crack and tumble the walls and spread ourselves across a rather pleasing mound where the house once stood and the sun will shine on us and the breeze lift our fronds and our roots will take the firmest purchase among the stones of the ruins.

JACK *gives an exhausted little laugh.*

JACK: It's good to be a dock plant, grandfather.
DICK: It is, lad.

(*Distant country sounds. They are abruptly cut by a door opening. Boots approach along a concrete path*)

JIM (*in panic*): He's coming.

(*Boots stop*)

DICK: He's stopped. He's leaning against the house wall. His ears have gone purple.
JACK: Ears?
DICK: Those two fronds besides his head.
JIM: They're always that colour.
DICK: Not that deep tint, Jim. Not quite that hue. Look, his head's drooping, he's sagging.
JACK: He is, uncle Jim, he's sagging.

(*Pause—country sounds*)

JIM (*in alarm*): He's straightened up now.
DICK: He's in pain.

(*Clank of metal*)

JIM: He's hoisted his tank. (*In panic*) He's spotted us.

(*Close: three footsteps in grass. Pump and hiss of spray. Droplets rattle loud and close on the leaves like rain hitting canvas*)

JIM
DICK } (*in alarm*): Ahhhh.
JACK

JIM: He's hit us.

DICK (*shouts angrily at man*): Get out of it. We'll wreck your house. We'll overrun you. We'll strangle your life out.

JACK (*frightened*): Oh grandad, grandad.

JIM (*in panic*): It's beginning to burn, it's burning.

DICK (*angrily at man*): The bullocks will bog on you. We finished the old one off. Get back in your cold frame where you belong.

JACK: Grandad, grandad.

(*Pump, hiss and drumming patter of spray hitting leaves*)

JACK
JIM   } (*in pain*): O-O-O.
DICK

JIM: We're finished, we're done for.

JACK (*wails*): Grandad. Grandad.

DICK (*suffering*): Hold on, lad, hold on.

JIM (*suffering*): I can't go through this again.

DICK (*suffering*): Hold on, Jim. Keep your roots tight round the limestone.

JACK (*wails in pain*): I've got no limestone, grandad, only soil.

DICK (*suffering*): Hang on in the soil then, Jack. Hang on in the soil, lad.

JIM (*in panic*): Here it comes again.

(*Pump, hiss and drumming patter of spray hitting them again*)

JIM
DICK } (*in pain*): O. O-O-O-O. O.
JACK

(*They gasp and groan*)
(*Clank of tank, boots move away*)

DICK (*suffering*): He's done here.
JIM (*suffering*): He's done for us.

> (*They all groan with pain, then suddenly* JIM *shrieks in panic*)

JIM: I'm swelling.
DICK: You're not.
JIM (*hoarsely*): I'm twisting, I'm climbing. What's this, what's this? It's the lichen. I'm up the wall top. (*More hoarse*) I'm dry, I'm dry, Dick. I'm choking.
DICK (*suffering, beginning to be hoarse and in a quietened voice*): Grip with your tap roots, Jim. Hold on to your limestone.
JIM (*hoarse and panting*): Can't, can't.
DICK: If you can. If you conceivably can, Jim.
JIM: It's all up. My number's up.
JACK (*weakly*): It hurts, grandad. It burns.
DICK (*hoarsely and struggling with his own pain*): Only a little burning, Jack lad. Like the sun.
JACK (*weakly*): Not like the sun, grandad.
DICK (*hoarsely*): It'll pass, Jackie, it'll pass.
JACK (*weakly and fading*): The autumn, grandad. I've never seen an autumn, nor known a winter in the soil.
DICK (*hoarsely but urgently*): Jack. Jack. Jack. Rouse lad, fight, hold on.

> (JIM *lets out a long hoarse moan*)

JIM: The aching, the aching. (*Groans*)
DICK (*hoarsely and weakly*): Hold on, Jim.
JACK (*weakly*): Grandad.
DICK (*weakly*): Hold on, son.

> (*Distant country sounds. Then a patter, continuous and much more gentle than the spray. It continues under dialogue*)

JACK (*weakly*): Grandad.

DICK (*in pain*): Son?

JACK (*weakly*): Grandad, there's something more falling on us now.

DICK: No, son. He's finished. There's nothing falling.

JACK (*weakly*): Grandad, it is. Grandad, it's the, it's the (*weeping and half laughing*) it's the rain.

DICK (*weakly and hoarsely, not believing*): Yes, lad.

JACK: It is, grandad, it is.

DICK (*hoarsely and surprised*): It is. It is. It is the rain indeed. The rain is falling.

(*The rain falls in the clear*)

JACK (*tired*): Oh grandad, oh grandad. The rain's so cool.

DICK (*makes sounds of suffering a pain which is becoming endurable*): Oo. Ah. Ehhh. Whee. Jim, Jim, Jim, the rain.

JIM (*feebly*): Where?

DICK: The rain, it's falling, Jim.

JIM: No rain.

DICK: It's falling, Jim. It's falling. It'll swill the pain away.

JIM: No rain.

DICK: It is, Jim.

JACK: Not on uncle Jim, grandad.

DICK: Everywhere.

JACK: Because he's in the shelter of the wall.

DICK: Jim, hold on, Jim. It'll drip on you in time.

JIM (*puzzled*): In time?

DICK: In short time.

JIM (*reminiscently*): I remember the beginning of time.

JACK: He's pale, grandad. He's contorted.

JIM: The house.

DICK (*comfortingly*): Yes, Jim.

JIM: The bullocks are stepping out of the chimney pots, the clouds are passing beneath the soil.

DICK (*urgently to arouse him*): Jim! Jim!

JIM (*quite calm now and lucid in a distant memory*): Dick.

What happened to Edward that grew in the incinerator?

DICK: That was long ago, Jim.

JIM: Was it?

DICK: Yes, long ago, Jim, in the very first season of this garden, only shortly after the beginning of time.

JIM (*having been answered*): Oh.

(*A metallic clatter*)

JACK: The person's dropped the tank, grandad. He's leaning against the house wall again.

DICK: He is. He is, Jim. His ears are purple. Jim, they're swelling.

JACK: And his toes, grandad, they're bursting out like melons.

DICK: Jim, Jim, listen, Jim. He's done himself in. The poison, Jim, he's poisoned himself with his pestilential cloud.

JACK: His limbs, grandad, they're writhing.

DICK: He's growing up the drainpipe like bindweed.

JACK: *He's* burning and swelling now, grandad. Will the rain avail *him*?

DICK: No, it won't. Jim, he's burning and swelling and the rain won't avail him.

JIM (*feebly*): My tap roots, my tap roots.

DICK: What, Jim?

JIM: Gone numb, can't feel them. I'm keeling over.

DICK: Not now, Jim. The rain will run on you any moment now.

JIM (*feebly*): Yes. (*He makes a weak sound of pain*)

(*The creaking and breaking sound of roots coming up through the soil is heard*)

(JACK *shrieks in panic*)

JACK: Grandad, the soil's cracking round uncle Jim's stem.

(JIM *groans feebly*)

(The roots continue to creak and break)

DICK: Jim, Jim. Just hold, Jim.
JACK: The earth's cracking, grandad. The little stones—

(A cascade of gravel)

JACK: And the worms and insects tossed into the daylight and *(cry of horror)*—
DICK: Look away.

(A final anguished groan from JIM)
(The final creaking of the roots and the sudden small shift of running earth and stones)

JACK *(soberly)*: Those were his tap roots, grandad, gone black.
DICK *(soberly)*: Yes.

(Fall of rain. Tinkle of rivulets)

JACK: And the person, grandad, his toes have burst. His head's gone black.
DICK *(exhausted)*: Bask in the rain, Jack.

(Rain and rivulets briefly in clear)

JACK: Are *you* all right, grandad?
DICK *(exhausted)*: I will be. I need more time than young 'uns.

(House door opened)

JACK: The other person, grandad. The other person's coming.

(Woman's footsteps on concrete path. They stop. At a higher note than we have heard from the plants the woman screams. The rain falls heavily and the rivulets flow. Fade.

(The rain has stopped. It is evening and the distant sounds of the bullocks, sheep and birds are more widely spaced. Doors of a vehicle bang. The vehicle drives slowly away. The conversation, at the end of a tiring day, is slow and reflective)

JACK: So that's what's meant by taking him away in the vehicle, grandad.

DICK (*restored but tired*): Honour's even at the end of the day.

JACK: Quite a nice evening, grandad.

DICK: We needed that rain.

JACK: You all right now, grandad?

DICK: Yes, fine. And you, son?

JACK: Fine.

DICK: We needed that rain, even without—ah well. (*He stops*)

(Distant peaceful country sounds)

JACK: Grandad, the other person and all the little persons they turned black.

DICK: They do when one of them dies.

JACK: But we aren't black, grandad, and uncle Jim's died.

DICK: It doesn't work the same way.

JACK: Am I mottled, grandad?

DICK (*laughs*): A bit.

JACK: Orange and purple?

DICK: Slightly. It'll pass. You'll come up fresh next spring.

JACK: And I'll be bigger then and better able to withstand things.

DICK: Yes.

JACK: I tried to be tenacious.

DICK: You were, son.

JACK: Am I intrepid, grandad?

DICK (*warmly*): You are.

(JACK laughs with pleasure)
(Distant country sounds, widely spaced. Separate bird

notes. Gnats are heard)

JACK: It seems a pity, though, doesn't it, grandad?

DICK: What, lad?

JACK: Well, we're never going to take possession of the house and ruin it, not really.

DICK: You can't tell.

JACK: And they're not ever going to finish the dock plants off.

DICK: They're certainly not.

JACK: It's a pity then, isn't it, grandad—encroachment and the spray, uncle Jim rotting there with his broken roots in the air and the person taken away in the vehicle.

DICK: I suppose it is.

JACK: Well, why do we do it, grandad? Why do they?

DICK: I suppose because it's natural, inevitable.

JACK: How, grandad?

DICK: I don't know, Jack . . . I did have an explanation of it once.

JACK: I see.

DICK: He should never have said what he said. He should never have likened me to a clump of rhubarb, he should never have said that.

JACK: No.

DICK: He'd become dried out growing under that wall.

JACK (*yawns*): Been a long day, grandad.

DICK: It has, Jackie. (*Pause*) Nice evening though now. Fresh.

JACK (*sleepily, in agreement*): Ah, ah.

DICK: Nice calm evening.

(*Separate distant bird notes*)

DICK: Grand night.

(*Owl hoots*)

DICK: Grand clear night beneath the stars.

CHARACTERS

LAURA LOGAN
MCNEE
MISS PARKER
MAX

Place
Laura Logan's flat in Marble Arch Mansions, W2.
Time
Friday morning.

MARBLE ARCH

LAURA LOGAN'S *flat near Marble Arch. Lots of wrought-iron furniture, white furry rugs, white leather chairs. Centre— the bedroom. A big double bed unmade, dressing table, etc, white TV. Door left leads to a bathroom and a lavatory. We can see a part of the bathroom floor and wall behind the shut door. Door right leads to a hall into which the flat's front door, and kitchen and sitting-room doors open. A tallboy in the hall beside a hall table.* LAURA LOGAN—*one-time toast of the Rank Organization, Queen of Pinewood and star of a dozen forgotten British movies —is on the bed, red hair and pearls in place, wearing a flowing black negligee and doing her slimming exercises. On a chair by the bed, a man's dark jacket, waistcoat and tie. By the bed, an opened bottle of champagne and two glasses, a tray with coffee and toast for two, half eaten. Around the flat, photographs of* LAURA *in low cut dresses, riding habits, etc, signed pictures of James Mason, Stewart Granger, Patricia Roc and Margaret Lockwood. She stops exercising and shouts at the bathroom door.*

LAURA: Max! Max! (*She gets off the bed, pushes her feet into furry slippers*) What's happened to you in there, Max? (*Shouts at the bathroom door*) Don't you have to be back downstairs by ten-thirty? Hurry up for heaven's sake! Your lady wife'll be back from bridge with her mother in Horsham, and all those sticky little drinks after dinner which stopped her driving back last night. (*She goes to the dressing table, starts brushing her hair*) Do you realize if it hadn't been for the breathalyzer, I'd never have the full glory of a whole night in bed with you once a week, Max? And your filthy pipe in my Charles of the Ritz cleansing cream! (*Doing her eyes*) For all these years—I only had you up to eleven-thirty Thursday evenings, and now—thanks to the inspiration of the Ministry of

Transport, you can stay until Friday morning . . . Big deal!
Big, enormous, sumptuous deal . . . (*She looks at the door
curiously*) Got a sudden attack of courage, or something? I
mean, you're not going to run the risk of letting Phyllis
find out, are you? (*Stops making up, talks to the door*) Did
I tell you, Max—I met your little Phyllis in the lift last
week? Really, I hardly noticed her against the beige of the
wallpaper . . . and she said 'Saw your old movie on the
telly last night, Miss Logan . . . Amazing to see those
movies now,' she said. 'Isn't it, Miss Logan?' (*She gets
up, goes to the bathroom, shouts at it*) Come on, Max! For
God's sake—are you going to spend all day in my loo, con-
templating . . .?

(*She moves back to the dressing table*)

I said 'No doubt movies always struck you as bloody amazing, particularly the arrival of talkies which must have come
as something of a shock to you—late in life' . . . Don't
worry, I didn't say that really . . . I mean, we couldn't say
that to little Phyllis, could we? Phyllis has to be taken care
of . . . (*She stands up and crosses to the champagne.
Picks up the bottle and shakes it, her hand over the top, to
restore the fizz*) And what do I get? Six nights a week on
my own, watching television. (*She picks up a glass*) The
Golden Years of the British Cinema! You won't even take
me out to dinner. Oh no! We can't be seen together! All
the portions of Israeli Melon and Coq au Vin and stuff en
croûte you never dared buy me in public. Well, at least I made
you pay for them, Max! One thousand and fifty-three
dinners at the Mirabelle in cash. In shoe boxes under my
bed! (*She stoops and pulls out a cardboard shoe box, opens
it, showing it's full of five pound notes—gestures with it
rudely at the door*) Don't you think that's humiliating for
me—having all my nights out in shoe boxes? You're a
coward, Max! What's the good of you owning two film
studios and thirty-three Orpheum Cinemas and Birming-

ham Weekend Television if you can't announce the take-
over of a human person?

(*The phone rings beside the bed. She stuffs the shoe
box back under it*)

Who the hell's that? (*She pours herself another glass of
champagne, drinks, picks up the phone and answers it in a
purring actress's telephone voice, gentler and more former
Rank charm school than the tones in which she has been
abusing Max*) Hullo? Yes. Yes, this is Miss Logan speaking
. . . (*She covers the mouthpiece and talks to the door*) It's
the BBC, Max. That's not one of yours is it? (*Uncovers
mouthpiece*) What? New Zealand Service? You want to
what . . .? You mean they've just got around to seeing
my films in New Zealand? Have they heard about the
Battle of Alamein . . . ? . . . Oh yes. Well, of course you
can interview me. Be delighted. From ten-thirty this
morning I'll be free until next Thursday evening. (*She
puts down the phone, says gloomily*) It seems there's a good
deal of interest in me, down under. (*She flops down on the
bed drinking champagne*) Interviews! It'll be quite like old
times. I had a career once, remember? The day you first
met me. Stage B at Shepperton, I was running down an
iron staircase with nothing on but a few stick-on
sequins and an arse full of feathers. 'Mignonette . . .
Follies Girl and Heroine of the Resistance.' Well . . . they
really wanted Margaret Lockwood. They got her after that,
didn't they darling? After you snatched me out of the
public gaze, and stuck me in the flat above you and
Phyllis so you could just creep up in the lift on
Thursdays! Swine Max! (*She sits down on the edge of the
bed, shouts at the closed door*) If you'd ever had the
decency to marry me . . . I'd bloody well divorce you.
(*She gets up, puts the glass on the bedside table, and
walks up and down, furious*) What's in it for me
. . . ? Sweating it out up here on massage and Easy Slim

Biscuits so I can always be little feather-tailed Mignonette when I want to be your wife with a coat and skirt from Debenham's Outsize Department and twin beds where we could lie reading until we fell quietly asleep, and didn't care who knew it. I'm fed up with all this secrecy! Who do you think you are, anyway? It's like having it off with the Pope or something. (*She stands in front of the bathroom door. Shouts at it*) I used to be young, Max. Can you hear me? I sat here on Monday, watching television. And there was I, a slip of a girl being raped by Stewart Granger, and I saw myself—all tear-stained with my lace jabot rudely torn away—and I said 'Cheer up, darling . . . there's worse in store for you! Buried alive. That's what you're going to be. By the Chairman of the Board!' Max! Max! (*Enraged, she beats on the door*) Why can't you answer? What's the matter with you? Have you dropped dead in there?

She turns the handle and pushes the door violently. Greatly to her surprise, it is not locked. It opens. She goes into the bathroom and looks. She stands for a moment, looking in horror.

Oh, Max . . . you have! (*Then she returns to the bedroom, shutting the door reverently. Long pause*) Max . . . my poor Max.

She goes to the bedside table, takes a cigarette out of a white alabaster box and lights it with her hand trembling. She sits down on the bed, facing the closed door, blowing out smoke. Long pause.

What do you think people are going to say . . . ? (*Pause*) I've got your reputation to think of. (*Pause*) Oh, Max . . . if you wanted to die, why couldn't you do it in your own flat?

(There's a ring at the front doorbell)

Who's that?

(The ring is repeated. She gets up slowly, looks despairingly at the bathroom door)

You'll get me thrown out of here, Max. Don't you know this place belongs to the Church Commissioners . . . ?

(The ring comes again. She moves out of the bedroom to the hall)

They even fuss if you get too noisy playing the Epilogue. Who is it?
MCNEE: It's me, Miss Logan.
LAURA: Oh, McNee . . .

She opens the door a crack. We can see a small segment of MCNEE, the porter, standing at the door. He has gold-rimmed glasses, a severe expression and a Scots accent.

MCNEE: I just brought up your things from the cleaner, Miss Logan.
LAURA: Thanks, McNee. I'll take it . . .

She opens the door a crack further, takes the cleaning, a couple of dresses on a hanger.

MCNEE: I'll be up in about five minutes for the rubbish, Miss Logan.
LAURA *(very nervous)*: I . . . I haven't got any rubbish today, thank you very much. *(She goes into the bedroom, puts the cleaning on the bed)*
MCNEE *(incredulous)*: No rubbish?
LAURA: No rubbish at all . . . *(She shuts the bedroom door)*

MCNEE: There must be rubbish in your tidy bin . . . Miss Logan. (*He pushes the door open and goes towards the kitchen*) (*Off-stage from kitchen*) I'll be back directly.

LAURA, *who hasn't heard him, goes through the bedroom to the bathroom, turns away her head as she opens the bathroom door a crack, gets out the key from the inside of the door, and shuts the door again and locks it on the outside, leaving the key in the lock. She starts to move towards the telephone.*

LAURA: Who do I ring . . . Dr Fruteman? (*She sits on the bed, the telephone on her lap. Looks at it*) Oh, Dr Fruteman . . . I think there's a man dead in my loo . . . (*She looks up at the bathroom door*) Max . . . How could you! (*She starts to dial. As she does so,* MCNEE *comes out of the kitchen and crosses the hall. To the phone*) Oh . . . Is Dr Fruteman in, please? . . . You expect him any moment? Could you ask him to give me a ring? It's Miss Logan . . . Laura Logan. (*Annoyed*) No, I won't spell it! It used to be a household word. (*She puts down the phone*) If only Dr Fruteman could find you passed away peacefully . . . in your own bed, Max . . . (*She puts the phone back on the bedside table. Moves towards the bathroom door and speaks at it*) Don't you see, darling . . . it'd be so much more pleasant. (*She moves round the room*) Well, it's only just downstairs . . . you'd only have to go down one floor to it. There's a lift . . .There's . . . a . . . (*An idea is dawning*) . . . a lift! (*She goes to the door and speaks to it quickly, persuasively*) It's just one floor, Max! But it'd make all the difference. All right?

(*No answer, so she answers herself*)

All right . . . (*She moves quickly to the telephone*) I'll need help, that's all. (*She looks at the telephone and then starts to dial*) Is that Harrods? Oh, could you give me your Removal Department please? Removals! You undertake all sorts of removals? I don't mean of anything . . . I mean of anybody. Alive or dead . . . Well, I'm trying to explain. It's simply a question . . .

(*Front door bell rings*)

Oh . . . I'll call you back. (*She slams down the telephone*) It's always the same! Mend my own fuses—fix my own drinks . . . (*Speaks to the bathroom door*) See what it's like, Max—being a woman on your own?

She goes through the bedroom door quickly, and shuts it behind her. She takes a deep breath, and opens the front door slowly. MCNEE *is standing there, with a rubbish disposal trolley. Two wheels and a long handle to which is fitted a large sack of reinforced paper, held open by a large circle of iron at the top and with a metal cover.*

MCNEE: Bring out your dead, Miss Logan!
LAURA: What? (*She moves back appalled as he walks past her. He stops to open the kitchen door. The rubbish disposal trolley between them*)
MCNEE: It's my wee joke, Miss Logan. Something I often say, when I'm collecting the rubbish.
LAURA: Very . . . funny!
MCNEE: Sorry to keep ringing. I left my pass key downstairs.
LAURA: That's all right.
MCNEE: Not disturbing you, I hope . . . ?
LAURA: Oh, not at all really. (*As he gets the trolley*) You've got a pass key, have you . . . ?
MCNEE: Downstairs . . .
LAURA: So you can get into any of the flats . . . ?
MCNEE: Oh yes. I have to. In case of accident . . .
LAURA: In case of accident! (*She looks at him hard*) Mr

McNee . . . You know the flat below here?

MCNEE: Number 4?

LAURA: Yes. Number 4 . . . Is the lady from Number 4 . . . back yet?

MCNEE: I don't think so. The car's not outside.

LAURA: I was just wondering . . .

MCNEE: Well, I'll just trundle this wee dustbin into your kitchen.

LAURA (*looks at the dustbin, fingers it thoughtfully*): It's not so wee, is it? . . .

MCNEE: What's not so wee?

LAURA: Your dustbin . . . ?

MCNEE: No . . .

LAURA: No. In fact, it's quite large. (*She opens the lid and looks into it*) And empty.

MCNEE: I made you my first call . . .

LAURA: You could get . . . quite a lot of rubbish in there.

MCNEE: It's surprising.

LAURA: Strong, is it?

MCNEE: Double thickness, wet-reinforced, ten-ply wood-pulp paper, you'd be surprised the objects it's had in it . . .

LAURA: Would I . . . ?

MCNEE: As I often say, you can know a tenant by his rubbish . . .

LAURA: I suppose you can. Mr McNee. (*She grips his wrist*)

MCNEE: Yes, Miss Logan?

LAURA: Please . . . (*She starts to pull him towards the bedroom door*) Just come with me for a moment.

MCNEE: I've no got the time . . . The regulation is—all rubbish out of sight be ten-fifteen a.m.

LAURA: He's strict, isn't he?

MCNEE: Who?

LAURA: Our landlord. Who is it—the Archbishop of Canterbury? (*She has got to the bedroom door—opens it*)

MCNEE (*as she gets him into the bedroom*): I'm told his Grace does keep a wee personal eye on the property.

LAURA (*she goes to the champagne bottle, shakes it to bring up the fizz*): And Marble Arch Mansions—was never touched by a breath of scandal.

MCNEE: Our reputation's untarnished.

LAURA : No suicides . . . no divorces. (*She pours out a glass of champagne for* MCNEE) Have a drink . . . And no pets!

MCNEE: Not during the hours of duty. Pets are not allowed.

LAURA (*advancing on him with the glass*): But all the same, they're here, aren't they?

> *During the following dialogue she comes nearer and nearer to him, threateningly.*

MCNEE: What's here?

LAURA: Pets!

MCNEE: Pets? (*Shakes his head*) Never! All animals forbidden, Miss Logan. (*He retreats from her, defensive*)

LAURA: Only in theory, isn't that so?

MCNEE: It's my personal responsibility . . .

LAURA: In the night-time, I hear poodles coughing.

MCNEE: . . . to see there are no animals on the premises . . .

LAURA: I've seen turtles going up in the service lift . . .

MCNEE: Well, you have to turn a blind eye occasionally!

LAURA: Exactly! (*She pushes the glass into his hand*) And how much does Mrs Montefiore pay you to keep quiet about her miniature Peruvian Apes?

MCNEE (*takes a quick drink from the glass of flat champagne*): It would be more than my job's worth.

LAURA: And what about the Guildersleeves in 6A?

MCNEE: What about them . . . ?

LAURA: If they're married, my name's Anna Neagle!

MCNEE: Some things are better taken at their face value, Miss Logan . . .

LAURA: And the two stockbrokers in Number 7!

MCNEE: Flatmates—From the landlord's point of view . . .

LAURA: And the sweet smell of Miss Cantor's cigarette is rare Egyptian tobacco, and those two married couples go into Number 9 every evening in full riding habit to play bridge.

MCNEE: You have to paper over the cracks once in a while, Miss Logan . . .

LAURA: Then paper over this one!

MCNEE: Which one?

LAURA: There's somebody dead in my bathroom.

MCNEE (*quickly empties his glass*): Somebody . . .?

LAURA (*moves to the bed, gets the bottle of champagne*): Dead.

MCNEE (*looks at her disapprovingly*): Oo . . . Miss Logan, you haven't . . .?

LAURA (*fills his glass*): Natural causes.

MCNEE: Is it someone you know?

LAURA: You know him too.

MCNEE: Who . . . ?

LAURA: The gentleman from Number 4.

MCNEE: But he's . . . a public figure . . .

LAURA: He has his private moments.

MCNEE (*lowers his voice*): You say he's passed over . . . ?

LAURA (*looks at the bathroom door, she speaks in a lowered voice also*): Yes.

MCNEE: In there . . . ?

LAURA: Yes.

MCNEE: But surely he's got a bathroom of his own . . . ?

LAURA: No doubt.

MCNEE: So what on earth . . . ?

LAURA (*suddenly aloud*): Oh, for heaven's sake, Mr McNee. You don't think he came up here just because he felt like snuffing out, do you?

MCNEE (*thoughtful*): No . . . I suppose he no did that . . .

LAURA: Life Peers don't seek this place out to die—like elephants!

MCNEE: Oo . . . Miss Logan. The landlords're no going to care for this . . .

LAURA: The landlords're no going to know.

MCNEE: It'll be in the papers . . .

LAURA: That he passed away in his own bed, while his wife was visiting her mother, and was found by their cleaning lady shortly before . . . eleven. That's when she arrives, isn't it?

MCNEE: What're you suggesting?

LAURA: Simply do your job, Mr McNee.

MCNEE: What job?

LAURA: Have the rubbish taken down. By ten-fifteen.

MCNEE: That's no a very nice way to refer to the gentleman.

LAURA: But that's what he is, at the moment. Don't you understand, Mr McNee? When you've taken him down to where he belongs, he'll be highly respected again. He'll be a force for good in the British Cinema, and the only Labour Peer to sell coloured television sets to Albania. And to me he'll be . . . well, he'll be how I always knew him. But at the moment—he's disposable.

MCNEE: I can't do it, Miss Logan.

LAURA: Are these service flats or aren't they?

MCNEE: Certain basic services—are provided.

LAURA: What could be more basic than this?

MCNEE: The Church Commissioners would nay like it . . .

LAURA: 'Lord Hammersmith found dead in wrong bathroom in Marble Arch Mansions' splashed all over the Daily Sketch. How's that going to tickle the Church Commissioners?

MCNEE (*doubtful*): We've always done our best, Miss Logan, to make you comfortable at the Mansions . . .

LAURA: Did I ever give you a Christmas Box? I rather . . .

MCNEE: I'm sure . . .

LAURA: I'm sure I forgot. Here . . . (*She moves quickly to the bed, feels under it and pulls the cardboard shoe box. She takes out a handful of money*)

MCNEE *looks at it, fascinated.*

Have some—of my dinner money!

MCNEE (*he holds out his hand, taking money*): I'm not sure . . . you didney forget Christmas . . .

LAURA: And your birthday! (*She puts more money into his hand*)

MCNEE: Down the service lift? It might be possible . . .

He holds out his hand for more money.

She puts the lid on the shoe box and puts it on the bed.

LAURA: Final instalment—when the place is all tidy.
MCNEE: It'd be a comfort. To the poor widow.
LAURA: To us all . . .
MCNEE (*moves towards the bed*): I'll do it for you, Miss Logan.
LAURA: I'm sure you will. (*Moving between him and the shoe box. She puts the shoe box quickly under the dress from the cleaners*)
MCNEE: I'll just slip down and get the pass key . . .
LAURA: Don't forget we haven't much time!

He goes quickly out of the bedroom and into the hall. He opens the front door of the flat and goes out hurriedly, failing to shut the door properly, so that it remains ajar. LAURA finds another cigarette, lights it. The telephone by the bed rings. At the same time the front door bell rings. She doesn't hear it. She picks up the telephone.

Yes . . . Yes, this is Miss Logan speaking. Oh, Dr Fruteman . . . how good of you to ring me back . . .

The front door is pushed open. A girl in a long footballer's scarf, wearing a duffle coat and carrying a tape recorder on a strap over her shoulder, comes in and looks round and curiously at the dustbin.

MISS PARKER: Hello, Miss Logan . . .
LAURA: Good-bye, Dr Fruteman.
MISS PARKER: I rang you from Bush House. Now, all ready for our little chinwag!
LAURA: Chinwag. I'm afraid that's out of the question now.
MISS PARKER: I'm thrilled to bits to meet you, Miss Logan. Is this your boudoir? Lovely. Listen, I wanted to take up the

acting line myself. As a matter of fact I was singled out for praise by the Auckland Star for my Mr Rochester in the Jane Eyre of Charlotte Brontë. But when they ask me what I've done, and I say Mr Rochester at Auckland High, it doesn't help much towards getting those female roles I long for. Now, where shall we go?

LAURA: Nowhere!

MISS PARKER: Well, I had to come to London after all I'd heard about the sweet life in Earls Court, so I just bummed my way half round the world. It makes a fascinating story if you've got a moment.

LAURA: I haven't. Not a moment. I've got the workmen coming in. I'm having the place done over.

MISS PARKER: But you clearly said on the phone this morning . . .

LAURA: That was another lifetime.

MISS PARKER: Are you aware someone's left a dustbin deposited in your lobby?

LAURA: Yes. Well . . . how ridiculous.

MISS PARKER: It does create a somewhat ratty impression.

LAURA: That shouldn't be there.

MISS PARKER: Want me to move it for you?

LAURA: No . . . No, I'll just put it in the kitchen . . .

MISS PARKER *switches on her tape recorder and speaks into it.*

MISS PARKER: One-two-three-testing. (*Deep voice*) I love you, Jane. Jane . . . We are free darling . . . (*To tape recorder*) My poor wife just burned to death in the west wing . . . (*She puts down the microphone on the hall table by the tape recorder*)

LAURA *comes out of the kitchen into the hall.*

LAURA: Miss Parker.

MISS PARKER: That looks better, doesn't it . . . ?

LAURA: Look . . . Miss Parker . . .

MISS PARKER: I never get round to tidying my own place this early either. Every morning my flat mate and I swear to God we'll get things shipshape before we go to work, but can we ever . . . ?

While MISS PARKER *and* LAURA *are speaking* MAX *crosses the strip of tiled floor and tries the bathroom door. He is a large man who looks stunned, having momentarily passed out on the loo. He's wearing a shirt with a wing collar only attached by a back collar stud and striped trousers with the braces hanging down. He tries the lock finding it locked and hearing* MISS PARKER'S *voice from the hall and he retreats again out of sight. At the same time* LAURA *has got hold of* MISS PARKER *and starts to push her out of the flat.*

LAURA: I'll have to ask you to go, Miss Parker, the fact is, I'm not feeling well . . .

MISS PARKER (*speaking at the same time*): Too bad . . . you're feeling crook?

LAURA: The doctor's on his way up now, to give me a thorough check up. (*She is opening the front door*)

MISS PARKER: Well, if you're not a hundred per cent . . .

LAURA: I'm not. (*She has got* MISS PARKER *through the door and out into the corridor*) Do ring me again. (*She starts to close the door on her*) Fix up another appointment.

She has the door closed. She leans on it for a moment, gives a sigh of relief and goes into the bedroom, picks up the champagne bottle, shakes it to make it bubble, pours out a quick glass and looks at the clock. MCNEE *opens the front door of the flat with his pass key. Comes in, his pass key on a big ring in his hand and looks for the trolley which he left in the hallway. Can't find it.* LAURA *goes to the bathroom door; turns the key so that* MCNEE *can remove* MAX. *As* MCNEE *reaches bedroom door, there is a violent ring at the front door of the flat.* MCNEE *looks at it, guilty and alarmed, not wanting to be found there on his curious errand. He opens the kitchen door and goes quickly into it, shutting it behind him.* LAURA *crosses the bedroom to answer the front door. She comes into the hall and shuts the bedroom door behind her. She opens the front door;* MISS PARKER *is standing there.*

I thought I told you . . .

MISS PARKER: Steady on, Miss Logan. I left my infernal machine!

MAX *appears again in the bathroom, still dazed and vaguely hooking up his braces. He tries the bathroom door again, finds it unlocked and emerges into the bedroom, He leaves the bathroom door open, puts on his coat and waistcoat, but leaves his collar undone and forgets his tie. Then he tiptoes with elaborate caution to the bedroom door, is halted by the sound of voices still continuing and he stands with his hand on the bedroom door handle, his ear against the door listening.* MISS PARKER *starts to pack her tape recorder.*

They'd've slaughtered me back at Bush House, if I'd left this behind. Anyway, I'll need it for my next assignment. At this very address as it happens . . . I'm interviewing a tycoon of considerable note . . .

Both LAURA *and* MAX *react to this.*

LAURA: A what?

MISS PARKER: Lord Hammersmith in person. I was booked for a chinwag with him and I thought as you lived in the same building and you still being such a name in Auckland . . .

LAURA (*appalled*): You're going down to Number 4 . . . ?

MISS PARKER: Right now.

LAURA: You can't do that . . .

MISS PARKER: Why not . . . ?

LAURA: Because . . . Because he won't speak to you . . .

MISS PARKER: Is he all that reserved?

LAURA: I've heard he's a very quiet man. Almost, totally silent.

MISS PARKER (*disappointed*): And I was hoping for a few tough words from him on the Sterling position—for the Dominions.

The kitchen door behind MISS PARKER's *head slowly opens, and* MCNEE *peers out. He gestures to* LAURA *pointing at his wrist-watch. She nods and grabs* MISS PARKER *by the wrist, and drags her towards the sitting-room door. At the same time* MCNEE *closes the kitchen door.*

MISS PARKER: What was that?

LAURA: Just my cleaning lady. (*She takes her arm*) Come in here with me. I'll give the Dominions something better than the sterling position.

MISS PARKER: Honest, Miss Logan?

LAURA: In the sitting-room. That suit you?

MISS PARKER: Too right! I promise you it'll be much appreciated.

LAURA (*opening the sitting-room door*): We won't be disturbed in here . . .

As LAURA *is moving* MISS PARKER *towards the sitting-room door which they are both facing,* MAX *opens the bedroom door a crack and peers out. Alarmed at seeing a strange woman in the flat, he retreats into the bedroom quickly. As he does so,* LAURA *gets* MISS PARKER *into the sitting-room.*

MISS PARKER (*on her way into the sitting-room*): How long can you give me, Miss Logan?

LAURA: Oh, just as long as it takes . . .

The sitting-room door shuts on them. This happens just at the same moment as MAX *has shut the bedroom door. At the same moment,* MCNEE *opens the kitchen door and comes out. He looks round the hall, makes sure the coast is clear and goes back into the kitchen to fetch his trolley.* MAX *opens the door a little, sees the trolley being moved towards the bedroom and then moves back and hides behind the bedroom door just as* MCNEE *opens it, and tramps straight through the bedroom, into the bathroom with his trolley. As soon as* MCNEE *is in the bedroom,* MAX *whips out of the bedroom and into the hall. He looks into the hall mirror and sees his tie is missing—starts to go back into the bedroom when the sitting-room door opens.* MAX *moves to hide behind the tallboy in the hall. At the same time* MCNEE *moves, looking puzzled, into the visible part of the bathroom.*

MISS PARKER (*OS*): Miss Logan, if you don't mind, I'll just get some of your pearls of memory down on tape. Half a mo . . .

MISS PARKER comes quickly out of the sitting-room, grabs the tape recorder from the hall table, and is back again as LAURA *appears at the sitting-room door. In the bathroom* MCNEE *is scratching his head.*

LAURA: Come back here . . . !
MISS PARKER: All set, Miss Logan!
LAURA: All right!

MISS PARKER goes into the sitting-room. LAURA *shuts the sitting-room door on both of them. In the bathroom* MCNEE *shrugs his shoulders and starts to move his empty trolley out.* MAX *is emerging from behind the tallboy in the hall when* MCNEE *bangs the bathroom door shut behind him. At this moment* MAX *quickly opens the kitchen door and goes into the kitchen.* MCNEE *walks straight through*

*the bedroom into the hall with his trolley. As he passes
the sitting-room door,* MCNEE *knocks on it and calls out.*

MCNEE: Your bathroom's all clear as far as I can see, Miss
Logan.

LAURA (*OS calls from the sitting-room*): Thank you, Mr
McNee . . . I'll speak to you later

MCNEE: I'll be back directly . . .

MCNEE *pushes his trolley out of the front door and bangs
the door of the flat shut.* MAX *then opens the kitchen door
and comes out into the hall. He hurries back into the bedroom to get his tie, sees it hanging on the chair and starts to
put it on leaving the bedroom door open. The sitting-room
door opens and* LAURA *comes out, she looks round nervously.*
MISS PARKER *comes out after her, her tape recorder slung
round her shoulder, holding out the microphone to catch*
LAURA*'s every word.*

LAURA: I'm sorry. My memory's rather short this morning.
They'll have to make do with that.

MISS PARKER: I was hoping you might have a little more for
your old fans, Miss Logan.

The bedroom door is open. MAX *retreats at the sound of*
MISS PARKER*'s voice towards the bathroom.* LAURA *moves
away from* MISS PARKER *towards the bedroom door.*

LAURA: Excuse me.

As LAURA *goes to the bedroom,* MAX *quietly shuts the
bathroom door. He stands on the strip of tiled floor as* LAURA
comes into the bedroom followed by MISS PARKER.

MISS PARKER: Perhaps we could get a bit further than your one
trip to Hollywood.

LAURA (*looks round the room*): Forgive me! It's been a morning . . . (*She sits down, tired, on the edge of the bed*)

MISS PARKER *comes close up to her, holding the micro-phone.*
MAX *puts his hand in his pocket, finds his pipe, takes it out and while he is waiting fills it from a tobacco pouch, sticks it in his mouth and finds a box of matches.*

MISS PARKER: I'd like a scrap or two on the purely personal level. If you feel up to it.
LAURA: On the personal level?
MISS PARKER: Your name's never been coupled with any romantic attachment?
LAURA: Is that of any interest, to my fans down under?

In the bathroom MAX *has got his pipe lit. He moves out of sight to throw the match down the loo.*

MISS PARKER: Why, stone the crows, Miss Logan, I'd say of absorbing interest. Was there any particular male at all concerned.
LAURA: Any particular male?

In the bathroom MAX *returns to view, blowing out smoke.*

MISS PARKER: That made any deep impression on you?
LAURA: There was, now you ask me, one lasting relationship . . .

MISS PARKER *kneels on the floor and holds the micro-phone out to* LAURA.

MISS PARKER: Could you say it again, a little closer to the mike?
LAURA: I am issuing this statement to you, Miss Parker, on the strict understanding it goes no further than the other side of the world . . .
MISS PARKER: You were married once . . .?

LAURA: Only on Thursdays.

MAX *waits, anxious at what she is going to give away.*

MISS PARKER: What? (*She holds the microphone closer to* LAURA)

LAURA: He only had time for me once a week, although I had time for him always. But on a Thursday, when his family was otherwise occupied in Horsham, he would slip up here and make what can only be described as love . . . (*She pauses*)

Still with his pipe in his mouth MAX *stoops down and listens, his ear to the keyhole, concerned, but also flattered at what he only half understands.*

MISS PARKER: Carry on, Miss Logan.

LAURA: He was the kindest man—and the most considerate lover. Love with him was like being handed gracefully into the warm, carpeted inside of a Daimler Hire. Our life together was not what might be considered exciting nowadays. I'd cook him roast lamb and rice pudding. His favourite programme was 'Come Dancing' and, more often than not, we'd be in bed before ten o'clock. But when we got there, it was extremely relaxed. There was a small vein in his forehead that pounded away when he read the 'Financial Times', and when I saw his head against the ribbons of my nightdress, that vein was quite still. He was an extremely clean man whose hands smelt of 'Wright's Coal Tar Soap'.

MISS PARKER: He sounds an almost perfect person . . .

LAURA: He had his weaknesses. Collecting—all manner of things. Old envelopes, bits of string, cotton reels, worn out rubber bands. He'd smooth out used brown paper and put it aside and say 'When the market falls this'll line my shoes on a wet evening'. He wouldn't go near the Embankment, on which he thought he'd end up sleeping.

MISS PARKER: What's happened to him now, Miss Logan?
LAURA: He's passed over.

> MAX *is listening in extreme astonishment, takes out his pipe.*

MISS PARKER: Recently?
LAURA: It seems—some time ago now. Of course, I attended the funeral . . .

> MAX *puts his still lit pipe into his jacket pocket as he hears this.*

MISS PARKER: Naturally . . .
LAURA: Incognito. Being neither family nor business, I sat between his numerous relatives and innumerable employees like a stranger. I refused, with dignity, the invitation to attend the large chicken dinner with which his departure was celebrated.
MISS PARKER: My oath! It must have been a most moving occasion . . .
LAURA: It was as he wanted it . . .

> MAX's *pipe has begun to burn his jacket pocket and the clouds of smoke are increasing rapidly.*

LAURA: No fuss and no flowers. Simply the band of the Salvation Army playing selections from Rodgers and Hammerstein . . .

> MCNEE *opens the front door with his pass key and comes into the hall, where he is stopped by the sound of voices from the bedroom.*

The Prime Minister was represented, and the urn was put where we always planned, with a view out all over Golders Green.

Suddenly MAX *notices that he is on fire and starts to slap wildly at his pocket to put himself out.*

I hope he's happy where he is now. He always had a strong fear of foreign travel.

LAURA *and* MISS PARKER *are silent. The front door opens,* MCNEE *comes into the hall.*
MAX, *who has failed to put himself out, moves further into the bathroom out of our view, to get water.*

MCNEE: Miss Logan . . .

Still wrapped in her golden memories of Max, LAURA *doesn't answer him.*
MCNEE *knocks on the bedroom door. The sound of his knock is drowned by the sudden rush of a tap and various crashes from the bathroom.* MAX *backs into our view in the bathroom again, sloshing water from a tooth mug over his coat.*
At the same moment, MCNEE *opens the bedroom door— sees* LAURA.

MCNEE: Miss Logan, I came up to report to you that . . . (*Sees* MISS PARKER)
LAURA (*looking amazed at the bathroom door*): Whatever . . .

She turns and crosses the bedroom to pull open the bathroom door. MISS PARKER, *her tape machine slung around her, has risen to her feet and* MCNEE *is following* LAURA *to the bathroom door of which they both have a full view as* LAURA *pulls it open to reveal the soaked and extinguished* MAX. MAX *turns and smiles at them both with a look of perfect calm and self-confidence.*

LAURA: Max!
MISS PARKER: Don't I recognize these famous features?

MCNEE: My lord! You are in the bathroom . . .

MAX: Good morning, McNee. 'Morning everyone.

MISS PARKER: Gee whiz. You wouldn't read about it. Is his lordship often to be found among your toilet facilities?

LAURA (*still amazed*): No . . .

MAX: No, of course not. I just popped up actually . . .

LAURA: You're alive . . .!

MAX: Alive? Of course I'm alive. It's not all that dangerous, you know. Fixing the plumbing. Gets you a bit on the wettish side, of course . . .

LAURA: Fixing the what?

MAX: I tell you, McNee, last night night I hardly slept a wink! I was kept awake by the pipes up here gargling like the Hallelujah Chorus! So this morning, tired out and exhausted, I called up and asked if I might personally inspect my neighbour's ball-cock. It was pretty gruelling work, I might say actually. (*Starts to pull a gold watch out of his waist-coat pocket. Then speaks to* LAURA, *with meaning*) I must've snoozed off in there for forty winks. Didn't want to burst in when you had visitors . . . (*Looks at his watch*) Good heavens! Is that the time? I must be trotting along. (*He moves towards the door.* MISS PARKER *is trotting after him like a small terrier*) I think that's solved your little problem, Miss Logan. I don't think you'll have any more trouble with your pipes.

MISS PARKER (*running after* MAX): Lord Hammersmith, Oh Hoo Roo, Miss Logan. Lord Hammersmith! My Lord, what do you think of the Sterling position?

MAX: The sterling position? What position is that my dear? (*He pats her bottom jovially as they go out of the door together*)

MAX *and* MISS PARKER *are out through the front door.* LAURA *is standing in the centre of the bedroom. Then she picks the dress up, to put it away, reveals the shoe box.* MCNEE *looks at it, she looks at him.*

MCNEE: There you are, Miss Logan, things are ne'er so bad as they are painted. There's no need to explain, Miss Logan. We must just see the landlord's asked no awkward questions.

> LAURA *gives* MCNEE *£10.*

Thank you, Miss Logan. I'll be up again tomorrow morning for your rubbish. As I often say—you can tell a tenant by her rubbish.

> LAURA *doesn't answer. He goes.*
> LAURA *is alone on the stage. She starts, listlessly, to tidy up. Then she stops and sits on the bed. Slumped inert. She gets out a cigarette, lights it. Then immediately stubs it out in the bedside ashtray as the phone rings. She is on her feet, eyes blazing, angry.*

LAURA: Max! Where the hell are you phoning from? Your kitchen. Where's Phyllis—not back? And Miss Down Under, oh she's in the lounge, is she . . . Listen to me—you're a coward, Max! A complete total one hundred per cent, terrified coward. You couldn't even die up here, could you? That's what I've got—a place you wouldn't be seen dead in. Wha . . . What're you talking about? Of course I'm not the Board of Trade. Oh, Phyllis has just walked into the room, has she? Well, why don't you tell her, Max? Why not . . .? You think I'm going to stay up here . . . like a prisoner . . . always? Oh . . . Oh Phyllis slipped out to the shops. What . . . what did you say? Oh, I suppose so . . .

> *The anger goes out of her suddenly.*

LAURA: All right, then. Yes, I'll be here . . . See you, Max. Thursday as usual. See you . . . lover.

> *She puts the phone down slowly. She picks up the stubbed-out cigarette, relights it with her lighter—sighs*

and goes slowly back to the routine of her everyday life. She goes into the bathroom.

Sound of water as she turns on the bath.

The Curtain Falls

Biographical Notes

SAMUEL BARCLAY BECKETT was born near Dublin on 13 April 1906. He was educated at Portora Royal School and at Trinity College Dublin, where he studied English, French and Italian. In 1928, when he was in Paris teaching English at the Ecole Normale Supérieure, Beckett met James Joyce, with whom he formed a lasting and important literary relationship. In the early nineteen-thirties he lived at various times in Germany, France, England and Ireland, settling in Paris in 1937. During the Second World War he worked with the French Resistance Movement; in 1942 he and Suzanne Dumesnil fled from the Gestapo to live in the Vaucluse in unoccupied France. They married in 1948. Beckett was Nobel Laureate for literature in 1969.

Since the war, Beckett has usually composed his works in French and later translated them into English. He has written poems, prose fiction and literary criticism as well as the plays which have earned him his world fame. His main novels are *Murphy* (1938), *Molloy* (1951), *Malone Dies* (1951), *The Unnamable* (1953), *Watt* (1953), and *How It Is* (1961). Among his shorter pieces are *Imagination Dead Imagine* (1965), *Lessness* (1969), *The Lost Ones* (1971) and *First Love* (1973).

Beckett's dramatic canon is characterized by the wide range of his formal experimentation. *Le Kid* (1931), in collaboration with Georges Pelorson, was written for performance at Trinity College; it was a fitting beginning for Beckett's career as a dramatist in that it parodied Corneille's *Le Cid*, the greatest French Neoclassical treatment of the concepts of Honour and Passion. *Eleutheria* (1947)—the word is Greek for 'freedom'—is Beckett's longest play; with an ironical use of the conventional three-act 'well made' structure, it portrays a young man's struggle to achieve his liberty, from his bourgeois context initially and finally from all context. His plan is to strive towards a condition of liberty 'by being as little as possible. By not moving, not thinking, not dreaming, not speaking, not listening, not perceiving, not knowing, not desiring, not being able, and so on'. Since these unpublished plays, Beckett has written two mime-plays (*Act Without Words*, I and II, 1956) and four radio plays (*All That Fall*, 1957, *Embers*, 1959, *Words and Music*, 1962, and *Cascando*, 1963). *Film* (1964) is Beckett's only piece for the cinema, *Eh Joe* was written for television, and *Breath* (1969) is a play without actors.

The stage-plays with speaking parts show a clear development from the rich texture of *Waiting for Godot* (1953) to the skeletal bareness of his 1976 plays *That Time* and *Footfalls*. Between these came *Endgame* (1957), *Krapp's Last Tape* (1958)—his first play composed in English—*Happy Days* (1962), *Play* (1963), *Come and Go* (1966), and *Not I* (1972).

Beckett is reluctant to comment on his writing, but he has published a few pieces of criticism which throw light on his creative work: *Proust* (1931) and *Three Dialogues with Georges Duthuit* (1949). Also of interest are the letters Beckett wrote to Alan Schneider when he was directing *Endgame*; these are to be found in *The Village Voice Reader*, edited be Daniel Wolf and Edwin Fancher and published by Grove Press, New York in 1963.

EDWARD FRANKLIN ALBEE was born in Washington DC on 12 March 1928. He was educated at Lawrenceville School, Valley Forge Military Academy, Choate School and Trinity College, Hartford, Connecticut. After his service in the US Army, he lived in New York and was variously employed in writing for radio, doing office work, selling books and records, and acting as hotel receptionist or as a messenger for Western Union.

From the beginning of his career, with *Zoo Story* in 1959, Albee's plays have been internationally popular and highly praised by critics. Among the many distinctions bestowed on his plays were a Tony Award in 1964 and a Pullitzer Prize in

1967. After *Zoo Story* came *The Sandbox* and *The Death of Bessie Smith* (1960); *Fam and Yam, The American Dream* and *Bartleby* (1961); *Who's Afraid of Virginia Woolf?* (1962); *The Ballad of the Sad Café* (1963); *Tiny Alice* (1964); *Malcolm*, *A Delicate Balance* and *Breakfast at Tiffany's* (1966); *Everything in the Garden* (1967); *Box-Mao-Box* (1968); and *All Over* (1971).

HAROLD PINTER was born in Hackney, in the East End of London, on 10 October 1930. At the local grammar school he was mainly interested in sport (sprinting, soccer and cricket) and acting (he played Macbeth and Romeo). In 1948 he went to the Royal Academy of Dramatic Art but left after two terms. His first published work was lyrical verse, and his first professional acting was on BBC radio. Early in 1951 he enrolled at the Central School of Speech and Drama, and in September he got his first professional stage employment with Anew McMaster's company touring in Ireland. In 1957 Pinter wrote his first play, *The Room*, in four afternoons between morning rehearsals and evening performances in a repertory company in Torquay: it was performed by students in Bristol. *The Dumb Waiter* and *The Birthday Party* were completed before the end of 1957, and these were followed by various revue sketches and *A Slight Ache* (1959), *The Dwarfs* (1960), *The Caretaker* (1960), *Night School* (1960), *A Night Out* (1960), *The Collection* (1961), *The Lover* (1963), *Tea Party* (1965), *The Homecoming* (1965), *The Basement* (1967), *Landscape* (1968), *Silence* (1969), *Night* (1969), *Old Times* (1971), *No Man's Land* (1975). Pinter has worked very importantly in the cinema, his main screenplays being *The Caretaker* (1963), *The Servant* (1963), *The Pumpkin Eater* (1964), *The Quiller Memorandum* (1966), *Accident* (1967), *The Birthday Party* (1968), *The Go-Between* (1971), *The Homecoming* (1971), *A la Recherche du Temps Perdu* (1973). A volume of Pinter's *Poems*, edited by Alan Clodd, was published in 1968, and issued in revised form in 1970.

TOM STOPPARD was born in Zlin in Czechoslovakia on 3 July 1937; he was brought up in Singapore and came to England in 1946. He was educated at Dolphin School, in Nottinghamshire, and Pocklington School, Yorkshire. He is married and has three children. He was a journalist from 1954 to 1963, at first working on newspapers in Bristol and then turning to free-lance journalism.

As well as the stage plays which have established his reputation, Stoppard has written for radio, television and the cinema. He has published one novel, *Lord Malquist and Mr Moon* (1966), and a volume of short stories, *Introduction 2* (1964). Stoppard's radio plays are *The Dissolution of Dominic Boot* (1964), *M is for Moon among Other Things* (1964), *If You're Glad I'll be Frank* (1965), *Albert's Bridge* (1967), *Where Are They Now?* (1970), *Artist Descending a Staircase* (1972). His screenplay *The Engagement* was completed in 1969.

Directly for the theatre, Stoppard has written *The Gamblers* (1965), *Tango* (1966—an adaptation of a play by Slawomir Mrozek), *Rosencrantz and Guildenstern Are Dead* (1966), *The Real Inspector Hound* (1968), *Enter A Free Man* (1968), *After Magritte* (1970), *Dogg's Our Pet* (1971), and *Jumpers* (1972). In 1973, *The House of Bernada Alba*, an adaptation of the play by Lorca, was produced in London. Stoppard's latest plays are *Travesties* (1974) and *Dirty Linen* (1976).

DON HAWORTH was born at Bacup, Lancashire on 18 January 1924 and went to Burnley Grammar School. He flew in the Royal Air Force and worked as a newspaper and television journalist in many parts of the world. He is now on the staff of the BBC in Manchester where he works as a TV documentary producer. Don Haworth would prefer to regard his true métier as that of a dramatist and primarily as a radio dramatist. He has had a play performed by the Hampstead Theatre Club, *A Hearts and Minds Job*, in 1971, and several other pieces have been done in lunch-time theatres and on television. His work for radio includes: *There's No Point in Arguing The Toss* (1967), *We All Come to it in The End* (1968), *A Time in Cloud Cuckoo Land* (1969), *The Prisoner* (1969), *Where is this Here Building—By What route do I Get There* (1970), *The Illumination of Mr Shannon* (1970), *Simcocks Abound Across the Earth* (1971), *The Enlightenment of the Strawberry Gardener* (1972), *The Eventful Deaths of Mr Fruin* (1972), *A Damsel and Also a Rough Bird* (1973). In 1972 the BBC published a book of Don Haworth's radio plays *We All Come to it in the End*.

JOHN MORTIMER was born in London on 21 April 1923. He was educated at Harrow and Brasenose College, Oxford. After working as an assistant director and then as a scriptwriter in the Crown Film Unit, he became a barrister in 1948. He is married to the writer Penelope Mortimer and they have three children. In 1972, he was drama critic for the *New Statesman*, the *Evening Standard* and *The Observer*. His novels are *Charade* (1947), *Rumming Park* (1948), *Answer Yes or No* (1950), *Like Men Betrayed* (1953), *The Narrowing Stream* (1954), and *Three Winters* (1956). *No Moaning at the Bar* (1957) and *With Love and Lizards* (1957) are his non-fictional prose works. Mortimer has written one Son et Lumière script, *Hampton Court* (1964) and one ballet scenario, *Home* (1968). For the cinema he has written *Guns of Darkness* (1962), *I Thank a Fool* (1962), *The Dock Brief* (1962), *The Running Man* (1963), *Lunch Hour* (1963), *Bunny Lake is Missing* (with Penelope Mortimer 1964), *A Flea in her Ear* (1964), *John and Mary* (1970). Mortimer's radio plays are *Like Men Betrayed* (1955), *No Hero* (1955), *The Dock Brief* (1957), *I Spy* (1957), *Three Winters* (1958), *Call Me a Liar* (1958), *Lunch Hour* (1960), *The Encyclopedist* (1961), *A Voyage round My Father* (1963), *Personality Split* (1964), *Education of an Englishman* (1964), *A Rare Device* (1965). For television, Mortimer has written *Call Me a Liar* (1958),

David and Broccoli (1960), *A Choice of Kings* (1966), *The Exploding Azalea* (1966), *The Head Waiter* (1966), *Hughie* (1967), *The Other Side* (1967), *Desmond* (1968), *Infidelity Took Place* (1968), *Swiss Cottage* (1972), *Knightsbridge* (1972).

Many of these radio and television pieces were later modified for stage presentation, and the following were first performed in the theatre: *What Shall We Tell Caroline?* (1958), *The Wrong Side of the Park* (1960), *Two Stars for Comfort* (1962), *The Judge* (1967), *Come As You Are*, comprising *Mill Hill*, *Bermondsey*, *Gloucester Road* and *Marble Arch* (1970), *Collaborators* (1973).